D1118677

TIME 100

TIME 100

Editor	Kelly Knauer
Art Director	Anthony Wing Kosner
Picture Editor	Patricia Cadley
Copy Editor	Bruce Christopher Carr
Designer	Scott G. Weiss
Production Director	John Calvano
Photo Technology	Urbano Delvalle
Time Special Projects Editor	Barrett Seaman

SPECIAL ISSUE STAFF

This book is based on two special issues of TIME. The editorial staff for those issues includes:

Managing Editor	Walter Isaacson
Editor, Heroes & Icons	Howard Chua-Eoan
Editors, Person of the Century	Howard Chua-Eoan, Philip Elmer-DeWitt, Stephen Koepp, Johanna Mc Geary
Picture Editor	Jay Colton
Art Director, Heroes & Icons	Marti Golon
Art Director, Person of the Century	Sharon Okamoto

Thanks to: Ames Adamson, Andy Blau, Anne Considine, Brian Fellows, Kevin Kelly, Emily Rabin, Betty Satterwhite Sutter, Michele Stephenson, Cornelis Verwaal, Miriam Winocour

TIME INC. HOME ENTERTAINMENT

President	Stuart Hotchkiss
Executive Director, Branded Businesses	David Arfine
Executive Director, Non-Branded Businesses	Alicia Longobardo
Executive Director, Time Inc. Brand Licensing	Risa Turken
Director, Marketing Services	Michael Barrett
Director, Retail and Special Sales	Tom Mifsud
Associate Directors	Roberta Harris, Kenneth Maehlum
Product Managers	Andre Okolowitz, Daria Raehse, Niki Viswanathan
Associate Product Managers	Dennis Sheehan, Meredith Shelley, Bill Totten, Lauren Zaslansky
Assistant Product Managers	Victoria Alfonso, Jennifer Dowell, Ann Gillespie
Licensing Manager	JoAnna West
Associate Licensing Manager	Regina Feiler
Associate Manager, Retail and New Markets	Bozena Szwagulinski
Editorial Operations Director	John Calvano
Book Production Manager	Jessica McGrath
Associate Book Production Manager	Jonathan Polsky
Assistant Book Production Manager	Suzanne DeBenedetto
Book Production Coordinator	Kristen Travers
Fulfillment Manager	Richard Perez
Assistant Fulfillment Manager	Tara Schimming
Financial Director	Tricia Griffin
Financial Manager	Robert Dente
Associate Financial Manager	Steven Sandonato
Executive Assistant	Mary Jane Rigoroso

Copyright 2000 by Time Inc. Home Entertainment
Published by TIME Books
Time Inc., 1271 Ave. of the Americas, New York, NY 10020
ISSN: 1521-5008
ISBN: 1-883013-64-X
We welcome your comments and suggestions about TIME Books. Please write to us at:
TIME Books
Attention: Book Editors
P.O. Box 11016
Des Moines, IA 50336-1016

To order additional copies, please call 1-800-327-6388
(Monday through Friday 7:00 a.m.–8:00 p.m. or Saturday 7:00 a.m.–6:00 p.m. Central Time)

All rights reserved. No part of this book may be reproduced in any form by any electric or mechanical means, including information storage and retrieval systems, without permission in writing from the publisher, except by a reviewer who may quote brief passages in review. TIME and the Red Border Design are protected through trademark registration in the United States and in the foreign countries where TIME magazine circulates.

Printed in the United States of America

TIME 100

TIME 100

H E R O E S & I C O N S

The Most Influential People Of the 20th Century

PERSON OF THE CENTURY

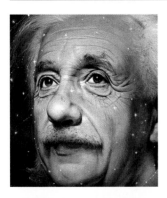

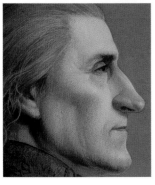

Foreword

The TIME 100

The two young men who founded TIME, Henry Luce and Briton Hadden, strongly believed in the power of the individual to influence history: week after week for many decades, the cover of the magazine always featured a portrait of a man or woman in the news. In the first issue of 1928, five years after TIME's debut, the editors named aviation pioneer Charles Lindbergh the "Man of the Year 1927." This designation of the individual who had done the most in the past year to affect the news for good or for ill became the magazine's signature journalistic act, the annual embodiment of its belief in the power of individual deeds to change the destiny of men and nations.

As the 20th century was drawing to a close, TIME managing editor Walter Isaacson conceived a project that reflected the magazine's deepest roots: to select and profile the 100 most influential people of the century in a series of special issues of the weekly magazine. The list would be divided into five groups of 20 individuals: Leaders and Revolutionaries, Artists and Entertainers, Builders and Titans, Scientists and Thinkers, Heroes and Icons. Noted authorities would be invited to write the profiles of the individuals named to the list. The entire project would culminate at the end of 1999 in the naming of a Person of the Century.

To select the 100 individuals, TIME solicited nominations from editors and journalists around the world, consulted outside experts and historians and registered opinions from millions of readers who sent in suggestions by mail and e-mail. The final selection was made in a series of occasionally contentious (but always stimulating) meetings that included journalists from CBS News, which produced a series of television specials on the project.

This is the third in a series of three hardbound volumes that collect the complete set of TIME 100 profiles. It features the final 20 individuals, the Heroes and Icons of the 20th century, and it completes the project by including TIME's selection of the Person of the Century—Albert Einstein—as well as two runners-up, Franklin D. Roosevelt and Mohandas Gandhi. The Person of the Century section also incorporates the TIME editors' designation of the most influential individuals for each of the previous nine centuries of the 2nd millennium. In transforming the special issues of the weekly magazine into book form, each story has been completely redesigned, and a number of new photographs, illustrations and related articles have been added.

TIME
100

Heroes

& Icons

Spirit of St. Louis

They thrilled us with their fervor, force and folly. And once they stretched the limits of the possible, we built new dreams from their designs

EVERLAST

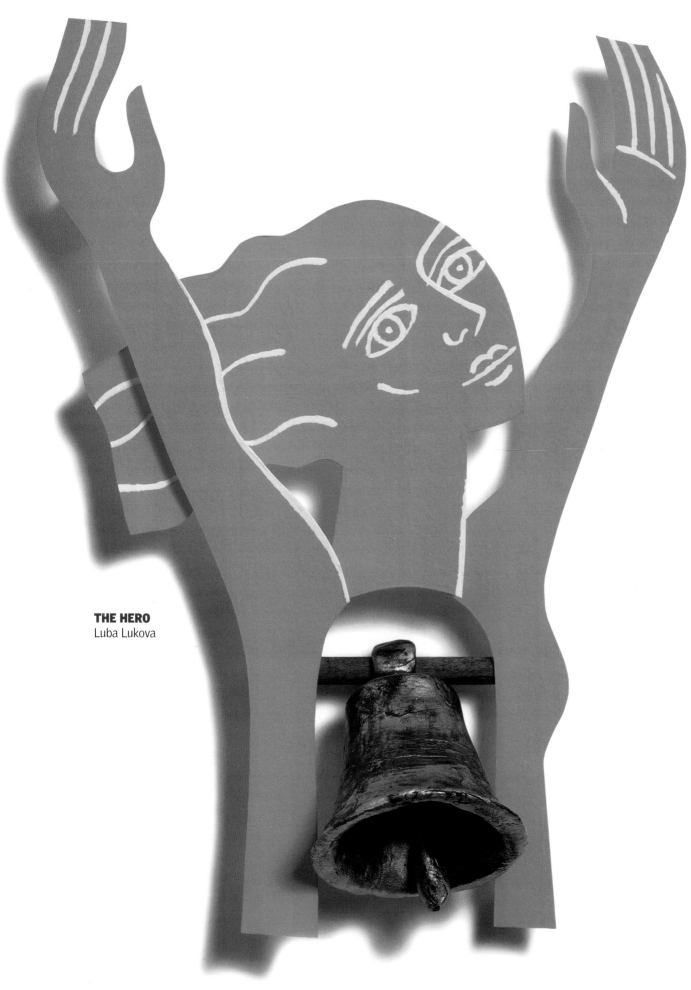

THE HERO
Luba Lukova

TIME 100

Embracing the Unattainable

By **HOWARD CHUA-EOAN**

The full moon, brilliant on a cloudless night, can humble even the most heroic of monuments. By Manhattan's Central Park, the seven American soldiers seem frozen in World War I. The men in the middle of the squad have bayonets ready for battle. One is injured but willing; another, caught in the arms of a comrade, is in the swoon of death. *Pro patria et gloria*—"For country and glory"—their motto reads in granite, barely legible. The infantry-men rise 15 ft. above the ground, an altitude that is micro-cosmic from the distance of the Sea of Tranquility. *Sic transit gloria?* As much can be said of the statue of Emmeline Pankhurst in London, her Edwardian gown antique against the constantly renewed moon, which has waned and waxed over her and other great men and women. It has lasted; they have gone the way of all flesh. Emmeline who?

Yet the moon is mute. And the magnificent swirl of the cosmos simply marks time: it cannot tell us of history, cannot instruct us on what to remember, what to proscribe, what to avoid. Memory is born of biological time, and it is borne on blood and bone and phlegm. Can the stars shudder at sacrifice? Only humankind can grasp the need for heroism amid the persistence of warfare simply by noticing that virtually across the street from the bronze soldiers, who fought a war spawned in the Balkans, is Yugoslavia's mission to the U.N. And only we can repent of forgetting that Pankhurst and her matronly, overlaced suffragists risked death for the right of women to vote. It is a blood debt.

We need our heroes to give meaning to time. Human existence, in the words of T.S. Eliot, is made up of "undisci-plined squads of emotion," and to articulate our "general mess of imprecision of feeling" we turn to heroes and icons—the nearly sacred modules of humanity with which we parse and model our lives. In this segment of the TIME 100, we have chosen a score who articulate the longings of the time they lived in. There are the extraordinary tales: of Andrei Sakharov's courage, Mother Teresa's selflessness, Marilyn Monroe's exuberance, Pelé's superhuman skills, Anne Frank's immortality. And the parables: the Kennedy melodrama, the latter-day silence of Muhammad Ali, the brutal grace of Bruce Lee's art, the all-too-human Diana, Lindbergh's dalliance with Hitler. Iconoclasm is inherent in every icon, and heroes can wear different faces in the after-lives granted them by history and remembrance.

Legend has it that the 8th century Chinese poet Li Po, drunk with wine, tried to embrace the moon reflected in a lake. He drowned in the clutch. He should have continued to embrace tales of flesh and blood instead of the surreal. For it is heroes—through their triumphs and follies—who teach us how to live. ■

Howard Chua-Eoan, an assistant managing editor of TIME, *supervised the Heroes & Icons segment of the* TIME 100.

Saipan, 1944: 3,426 U.S. soldiers were killed taking the island from Japan

The American G.I.

From disparate roots but united by patriotism, U.S. soldiers fought for freedom around the world

By COLIN POWELL

France, 1918: U.S. troops fire at German machine-gun nests

AS CHAIRMAN OF THE JOINT CHIEFS OF STAFF, I often referred to the men and women of the armed forces as "G.I.s." It got me in trouble with some of my colleagues at the time. Several years earlier, the Army had officially excised the term as an unfavorable characterization derived from the designation "government issue." Sailors and Marines wanted to be known as sailors and Marines. Airmen, notwithstanding their origins as a rib of the Army, wished to be called simply airmen. Collectively, they were blandly referred to as "service members."

I persisted in using G.I.s and found I was in good company. Newspapers and television shows used it all the time. The most famous and successful government education program was known as the G.I. Bill, and it still uses that title for a newer generation of veterans. When you added one of the most common boy's names to it, you got G.I. Joe, and the name of the most popular boy's toy ever, the G.I. Joe action figure. And let's not forget G.I. Jane.

G.I. is a World War II term that two generations later continues to conjure up the warmest and proudest memories of a noble war that pitted pure good against pure evil— and good triumphed. The victors in that war were the American G.I.s, the Willies and Joes, the farmer from Iowa and the steelworker from Pittsburgh who stepped off a landing craft into the hell of Omaha Beach. The G.I. was the wisecracking kid Marine from Brooklyn who clawed his way up a deadly hill on a Pacific island. He was a black fighter pilot escorting white bomber pilots over Italy and Germany, proving that skin color had nothing to do with skill or courage. He was a Japanese-American infantryman released from his own country's concentration camp to join the fight. She was a nurse relieving the agony of a dying

1898 T.R.'s Rough Riders are the advance guard of the 20th century G.I.

1941 Japanese attack on Pearl Harbor hurls U.S. into World War II

1945 U.S., Allies defeat Japan in Pacific

1965-72 Grunts endure peak years of long, divisive conflict in Vietnam

1991 Desert Storm: U.S. leads allies against Iraq

1898

1917-18 U.S. doughboys fight Germans in Europe

1950-53 G.I.s fight in tough "police action" in Korea

1944 D-day landing leads to Allied victory in Europe

1983 241 U.S. Marines killed by terrorist bomb in Lebanon

1999 U.S. and NATO troops defend Kosovo

> ## If it weren't for the American soldier, we would not have the freedom that we enjoy today.
>
> **HILLARY RODHAM CLINTON, nominating the G.I. as TIME's Person of the Century**

Vietnam, 1966: After a brutal firefight, Marine gunnery sergeant Jeremiah Purdue, center, reaches for an injured comrade at Hill 484, south of the DMZ

teenager. He was a petty officer standing on the edge of a heaving aircraft carrier with two signal paddles in his hands, fighting the elements as he helped guide a dive-bomber pilot back onto the deck.

They were America. They reflected our diverse origins. They were the embodiment of the American spirit of courage and dedication. They were truly a "people's army," going forth on a crusade to save democracy and freedom, to defeat tyrants, to save oppressed peoples and to make their families proud of them. They were the Private Ryans, standing firm in the thin red line.

For most of those G.I.s, World War II was the adventure of their lifetime. Nothing they would ever do in the future would match their experiences as the warriors of democracy, saving the world from its own insanity. You can still see them in every Fourth of July color guard, their gait faltering but ever proud.

Their forebears went by other names: doughboys, Yanks, buffalo soldiers, Johnny Rebs, Rough Riders. But "G.I." will be forever lodged in the consciousness of our nation to apply to them all. The G.I. carried the value system of the

American people. The G.I.s were the surest guarantee of America's commitment. For more than 200 years, they answered the call to fight the nation's battles. They never went forth as mercenaries on the road to conquest. They went forth as reluctant warriors, as citizen soldiers.

They were as gentle in victory as they were vicious in battle. I've had survivors of Nazi concentration camps tell me of the joy they experienced as the G.I.s liberated them: America had arrived! I've had a wealthy Japanese businessman come into my office and tell me what it was like for him as a child in 1945 to await the arrival of the dreaded American beasts, and instead meet a smiling G.I. who gave him a Hershey's bar. In thanks, the businessman was donating a large sum of money to the USO. After thanking him, I gave him as a souvenir a Hershey's bar I had autographed. He took it and began to cry.

The 20th century can be called many things, but it was most certainly a century of war. The American G.I.s helped defeat fascism and communism. They came home in triumph from the ferocious battlefields of World Wars I and II. In Korea and Vietnam they fought just as bravely as any of their predecessors, but no triumphant receptions awaited them at home. They soldiered on through the twilight struggles of the cold war and showed what they were capable of in Desert Storm. The American people took them into their hearts again.

In this century hundreds of thousands of G.I.s died to ensure that democracy is the ascendant political system on the face of the earth as we begin the 21st century. The G.I.s were willing to travel far away and give their lives, if necessary, to secure the rights and freedoms of others. Only a nation such as ours, based on a firm moral foundation, could make such a request of its citizens. And the G.I.s wanted nothing more than to get the job done and then return home safely. All they asked for in repayment from those they freed was the opportunity to help them become part of the world of democracy—and just enough land to bury their fallen comrades, beneath simple white crosses and Stars of David.

The volunteer G.I.s of today stand watch in Korea, the Persian Gulf, Europe and the dangerous terrain of the Balkans. We must never see them as mere hirelings, off in a corner of our society. They are our best, and we owe them our full support and our sincerest thanks.

As this century closes, we look back to identify the great leaders and personalities of the past 100 years. We do so in a world still troubled but full of promise. That promise was gained by the young men and women of America who fought and died for freedom. Near the top of any listing of the most important people of the 20th century must stand, in singular honor, the American G.I. ∎

General Colin Powell, former Chairman of the Joint Chiefs of Staff, now heads the volunteer corps America's Promise.

Korea, 1950: Under attack, a Marine finds he is out of ammo

Iraq, 1991: Mourning a friend, dead in the body bag at right

Charles Lindbergh

A new kind of hero for a new century, he became the unwitting pioneer of the age of mass-media celebrity

By REEVE LINDBERGH

I WAS THE YOUNGEST OF FOUR BROTHERS AND TWO sisters and grew up during the second half of my father's life, when the early years of triumph, tragedy and controversy were over. I felt no personal familiarity with the famous 1927 flight, and if I asked my father about that accomplishment, he would say only, "Read my book!"

He wrote this passage on the flight: "Now I've burned the last bridge behind me. All through the storm and darkest night, my instincts were anchored to the continent of North America, as though an invisible cord still tied me to its coasts. In an emergency—if the ice-filled clouds had merged, if oil pressure had begun to drop, if a cylinder had started missing—I would have turned back toward America and home. Now, my anchor is in Europe: on a continent I've never seen ... Now, I'll never think of turning back."

Sometimes, though, I wonder whether he would have turned back if he'd known the life he was headed for.

My father Charles Lindbergh became an American hero when he was 25 years old. After he made the first nonstop solo flight from New York to Paris in 1927, in a tiny silver monoplane called *Spirit of St. Louis*, his very existence took on the quality of myth. Overwhelming, overnight celebrity followed him home from Paris to the U.S. and around the nation on his tour promoting aviation. Fame followed him on his goodwill tour to Mexico late in 1927, where he met the U.S. ambassador's daughter Anne Morrow, who mar-

After the flight, 150,000 greeted Lindbergh on a London stop

ried him in 1929. They traveled all over the world as pioneer aviator-explorers, mapping air routes for the fledgling airline industry. Together they navigated by the stars and watched the great surfaces of the earth revealed beneath their wings: desert and forest and jungle and tundra, wild rivers and wide-open oceans. Land, sea and air: all of it seemed to be endless; all of it seemed to be theirs.

On the ground, my parents were dogged by the media,

BORN Feb. 4 in Detroit

1902

LINDBERGH, age 11, with his dog Dingo

1923 First solo flight

1926 Hired as airmail pilot

1927 Flies *Spirit of St. Louis* alone across the Atlantic

1932 His son Charles is kidnapped and found dead

1935 Bruno Hauptmann is convicted of the murder

1941 Resigns Air Corps commission, then is denied reinstatement after U.S. enters World War II

1954 Memoir of famous flight wins Pulitzer Prize

1974

DIES Aug. 26 in Maui, Hawaii

> ## Science, freedom, beauty, adventure: what more could you ask of life? Aviation combined all the elements I loved.

CHARLES LINDBERGH

Lindbergh responds to a crowd at the U.S. embassy in Paris after the flight

and they believed the excesses of the press were responsible for the kidnapping and death of their first son Charles in 1932. They withdrew to Europe to protect the children born after the tragedy, and returned to the U.S. just before World War II. My father then joined the isolationist America First movement, becoming a leader in the effort to keep the U.S. from entering what was seen by many Americans as a European war.

At odds with President Roosevelt and the interventionists, my father was branded a traitor, a Copperhead and even a Nazi. When he traveled to Germany to review German air power at the request of the American military attaché in Berlin, he was given a medal by his Nazi hosts and later ignored public appeals to repudiate and return it. (He had in fact sent it to a museum, as he did other awards he received throughout his life.) Finally, and disastrously, my father made a speech in Des Moines, Iowa, in 1941, identifying as the three groups unwisely advocating U.S. entry into the war "the British, the Roosevelt Administration and the Jews."

I was virtually unaware of my father's prewar isolationism until I went to college and was shocked to learn that he was considered anti-Semitic. I had never thought of him this way. He never spoke with hatred or resentment against any groups or individuals, and in social discourse he was unfailingly courteous, compassionate and fair. In the 1941 speech, however, I could read a chilling distinction in his mind between Jews and other Americans. This was something I did not recognize in the father I knew, something I had been taught to condemn under the heading "discrimination," something from another time.

The U.S. entered the war, and one hero's tarnished reputation did not mean much in the context of the unspeakable horror of the Holocaust or the wartime destruction visited upon the world. My father released a statement saying, "Now [war] has come and we must meet it as united Americans." He was denied an Army commission but found work as an adviser to Henry Ford, building warplanes at Willow Run, and as a civilian consultant to fighter pilots in the Pacific. By 1945, the year I was born, my parents were trying to leave the past behind them, and they bought a house in Connecticut to raise their family in peace and privacy. I never knew my brother Charles, but I felt the effect of his loss in the studied privacy and anonymity of our Connecticut suburb, with its shaded streets and unmarked mailboxes.

I am touched by the enormity of my father's accomplishment in its effect upon both those who witnessed it and those whom it inspired. People still tell me exactly where they were standing when they heard the news of his landing in Paris. Generations of pilots still talk of his influence upon their careers. I am moved again by people who remember the kidnapping and death of my brother, recalling their own fears as children or their compassion for my parents' loss. I have talked to prewar isolationists too, who defend my father's political position as an honorable one, even while feeling the distress I have felt about some of his speeches and writings.

He almost never talked to me about the past, because he lived so intensely in the present, never turning back. He did talk a great deal about newer concerns, chief among them the urgent need for balance between technological advancement and environmental preservation. When I knew him best, late in his life, he was flying around the world again, as he had done in the early days, but this time on behalf of endangered species, wild places and vanishing tribal peoples. He believed the aviation technology he loved was partly responsible for the devastation wrought by modern warfare and the degradation of the natural environment. "If I had to choose," he said, "I would rather have birds than airplanes," and he worked to promote an ethic in which birds and planes could continue to coexist.

My father was born with this century, grew up with it and experienced both its adventures and its excesses as few other human beings have done. He came of age with his country and his era and reflected both in many ways—not all of them, perhaps, entirely heroic. Yet my father, through intense public and private struggle, acquired over time a kind of reflective wisdom that took him far beyond his early fame. His journey through this century may have made him a greater hero in his quiet final years than he was in the tumultuous, triumphant days of 1927. ∎

Reeve Lindbergh's memoir of her family life, Under a Wing, *was published in 1998.*

Legends of the Air

In a century defined by flight, pioneers of the skies became modern-day folk heroes

Amelia Earhart

She was the first woman to fly the Atlantic solo; her disappearance in the Pacific during a round-the-world flight is an enduring mystery.

Piccard & Jones

Capping the century by breaking one of flight's last barriers, Bertrand Piccard of Switzerland and Brian Jones of Britain took their *Breitling Orbiter 3* balloon around the globe in 20 days early in 1999.

Chuck Yeager

One of the most gifted pilots in history, he first broke the sound barrier in the Bell X-1 *Glamorous Glennis* on Oct. 14, 1947.

Beryl Markham

In 1936 she became the first person to fly solo across the Atlantic from east to west. Her autobiography, *West with the Night*, is a classic.

Hillary & Tenzing

By conquering Everest, the beekeeper and the Sherpa affirmed the power of humble willpower —and won one for underdogs everywhere

By JAN MORRIS

ON MAY 29, 1953, EDMUND HILLARY of New Zealand and Tenzing Norgay of Nepal became the first human beings to conquer Mount Everest—Chomolungma, to its people—at 29,028 ft. the highest place on earth. By any rational standards, this was no big deal. Aircraft had long before flown over the summit, and within a few decades literally hundreds of people from many nations would climb Everest too. And what is particularly remarkable, anyway, about getting to the top of a mountain?

Geography was not furthered by the achievement, scientific progress was scarcely hastened, and nothing new was discovered. Yet the names of Hillary and Tenzing went instantly into all languages as the names of heroes, partly because they really were men of heroic mold but chiefly because they represented so compellingly the spirit of their time. The world of the early 1950s was still a little punch-drunk from World War II, which had ended less than a decade before. Everything was changing. Great old powers were falling, virile new ones were rising, and the huge, poor mass of Asia and Africa was stirring into self-awareness. Hillary and Tenzing went to the Himalayas under the auspices

of the British Empire, then recognizably in terminal decline. The expedition was the British Everest Expedition, 1953, and it was led by Colonel John Hunt, the truest of true English gentlemen. It was proper to the historical moment that one of the two climbers immortalized by the event came from a remote former colony of the Crown and the other from a nation that had long served as a buffer state of the imperial Raj.

I am sure they felt no zeitgeist in them when they labored up the last snow slope to the summit. They were both very straightforward men. Tenzing was a professional mountaineer from the Sherpa community of the Everest foothills. After several expeditions to the mountain, he certainly wanted to get to the top for vocational reasons, but he also planned to deposit in the highest of all snows some offerings to the divinities that had long made Chomolungma sacred to his people. Hillary was by profession a beekeeper, and he would have been less than human if he had not occasionally thought, buckling his crampons, that reaching the summit would make him famous.

They were not, though, heroes of the old epic kind, dedicated to colossal purposes, tight of jaw and stiff of upper lip. That was George Mallory, who said most famously in

> **"** Even on top of Everest, I was still looking at other mountains and thinking of how to climb them. **"**
>
> SIR EDMUND HILLARY, in a 1993 SPORTS ILLUSTRATED interview

The odd couple celebrate their peak experience in Katmandu

The real point of mountain climbing, as of most hard sports, is that it voluntarily tests the human spirit against the fiercest odds, not that it achieves anything more substantial—or even wins the contest, for that matter. For the most part, its heroism is of a subjective kind. It was the fate of Hillary and Tenzing, though, to become very public heroes indeed, and it was a measure of the men that over the years they truly grew into the condition. Perhaps they thought that just being the first to climb a hill was no qualification for immortality, for they both became, over time, representatives not merely of their own nations but of half of humanity. They came to stand for the small nations of the world, the young ones, the tucked-away and the up-and-coming.

BOTH, OF COURSE, WERE SHOWERED WITH WORLDLY honors, and accepted them with aplomb. Both became the most celebrated citizens of their respective countries and went around the world on their behalf. But both devoted much of their lives to the happiness of an archetypically unprivileged segment of mankind: the Sherpas, Tenzing's people, true natives of the Everest region. Tenzing, who died in 1986, became their charismatic champion and a living model of their potential. Grand old Ed Hillary, who is still robustly with us, has spent years in their country supervising the building of airfields, schools and hospitals and making the Sherpas' existence better known to the world. Thus the two of them rose above celebrity to stand up for the unluckier third of humanity, who generally cannot spare the time or energy, let alone the money, to mess around in mountains.

1924 that he was climbing Mount Everest "because it is there." But if he ever reached the summit, he never lived to tell the tale. Hillary and Tenzing were two cheerful and courageous fellows doing what they liked doing, and did best, and they made an oddly assorted pair. Hillary was tall, lanky, big-boned and long-faced, and he moved with an incongruous grace, rather like a giraffe. He habitually wore on his head a homemade cap with a cotton flap behind, as seen in old movies of the French Foreign Legion. Tenzing was by comparison a Himalayan fashion model: small, neat, rather delicate, brown as a berry, with the confident movements of a cat. Hillary grinned; Tenzing smiled. Hillary guffawed; Tenzing chuckled. Neither of them seemed particularly perturbed by anything; on the other hand, neither went in for unnecessary bravado.

As it happened, their enterprise involved no great sacrifice. Nobody was killed, maimed or even frostbitten during the British Everest Expedition, 1953. It was true to the temper of their adventure that Hillary's first words when he returned from the summit, to his fellow Kiwi George Lowe, were "Well, George, we've knocked the bastard off!"

I liked these men very much when I first met them on the mountain nearly a half-century ago, but I came to admire them far more in the years that followed. I thought their brand of heroism—the heroism of example, the heroism of debts repaid and causes sustained—far more inspiring than the gung-ho kind. Did it really mean much to the human race when Everest was conquered for the first time? Only because there became attached to the memory of the exploit, in the years that followed, a reputation for decency, kindness and stylish simplicity. Hillary and Tenzing fixed it when they knocked the bastard off. ∎

Jan Morris accompanied the British Everest Expedition, 1953. Her next book will be about Abraham Lincoln.

BORN Tenzing, May 1914, in Solo Khumbu, Nepal; Hillary, July 20, 1919, in Auckland, New Zealand

1953 Hillary and Tenzing are the first to reach the summit of Mount Everest

1984-89 Hillary serves as New Zealand's high commissioner in New Delhi

1914

1935 Charles Warren and Tenzing, his Sherpa porter, fail to summit Everest; Warren later introduces Tenzing to Hillary

1954 Tenzing becomes head of the Institute of Mountaineering in Darjeeling, India

DIED Tenzing, on May 9, 1986, in Darjeeling

The Great Explorers: "Because It's There"

Today space is "the final frontier," but early in the century, one could still set forth boldly for terra incognita

Roald Amundsen

In 1911 the Norwegian outraced Briton Robert Falcon Scott to the South Pole, beating him by a month. Scott and four members of his team died on the return journey, only miles from safety.

George Mallory

Controversy still swirls over whether he reached Mount Everest's peak in 1926. He did not live to tell the tale, and the stunning discovery of his body high on the mountain in 1999 left us asking: did he die going up, or coming back down?

Richard Byrd

The bold U.S. Navy Admiral was a pioneer of two frontiers, aviation and the antipodes. In the 1920s he became the first to fly over both the North and South poles.

Robert Peary

The American explorer said he was the first to reach the North Pole, in 1909, but Frederick Church, also an American, disputed his claim. Now some say neither of them reached the Pole.

Anne
Frank

With a diary kept in a secret attic, she braved the Nazis and lent a searing voice to the fight for human dignity

By ROGER ROSENBLATT

ALONG WITH EVERYTHING else she has come to represent, Anne Frank symbolizes the power of a book. Because of the diary she kept between 1942 and 1944, in the secret upstairs annex of an Amsterdam warehouse where she and her family hid until the Nazis found them, she became the most memorable figure to emerge from World War II—besides Hitler, of course, who also proclaimed his life and his beliefs in a book. In a way, the Holocaust began with one book and ended with another. Yet it was Anne's that finally prevailed—a beneficent and complicated work outlasting a simple and evil one—and that secured to the world's embrace the second most famous child in history.

So stirring has been the effect of the solemn-eyed, cheerful, moody, funny, self-critical, other-critical teenager on those who have read her story that it became a test of ethics to ask a journalist, If you had proof the diary was a fraud, would you expose it? The point was that there are some stories the world so needs to believe that it would be profane to impair

A bookcase hid the entrance to the attic in which the Franks took refuge

their influence. All the same, the Book of Anne has inspired a panoply of responses—plays, movies, documentaries, biographies, a critical edition of the diary—all in the service of understanding or imagining the girl or, in some cases, of putting her down.

"Who Owns Anne Frank?" asked novelist Cynthia Ozick, in an article that holds up the diary as a sacred text and condemns any tamperers. The passions the book ignites suggest that everyone owns Anne Frank, that she has risen above the Holocaust, Judaism, girlhood and even goodness and become a totemic figure of the modern world—the moral individual mind beset by the machinery of destruction, insisting on the right to live and question and hope for the future of human beings.

When the Nazis invaded Holland, the Frank family, like all Jewish residents, became victims of a systematically constricting universe. First came laws that forbade Jews to enter into business contracts. Then books by Jews were burned. Then there were the so-called Aryan laws, affecting intermarriage. Then Jews were

BORN June 12 in Frankfurt, Germany

1942 Receives diary for 13th birthday

1944 The Franks are captured by the Nazis and sent to Auschwitz

1947 Her father Otto has *Anne Frank: The Diary of a Young Girl* published

1929 **1945**

1934 Family moves to Amsterdam

1942 Anne's sister is ordered to report to the Nazis; the family goes into hiding

DIES in March of typhus in the Bergen-Belsen concentration camp

1955 Diary adapted as stage play

1995 Diary passages suppressed by Otto Frank are made public

"I wouldn't be able to write that kind of thing anymore ... Deep down I know I could never be that innocent again."

ANNE FRANK, in a comment added in 1944 to her diary entry of Nov. 2, 1942

A normal, if gifted, young girl: Anne Frank, around 1941

barred from parks, beaches, movies, libraries. By 1942 they had to wear yellow stars stitched to their outer garments. Then phone service was denied them, then bicycles. Trapped at last in their homes, they were "disappeared."

At which point Otto and Edith Frank, their two daughters Margot and Anne and the Van Pels family decided to disappear themselves, and for the two years until they were betrayed, led a life reduced to hidden rooms. But Anne had an instrument of freedom in an autograph book she had received for her 13th birthday. She wrote in an early entry, "I hope that you will be a great support and comfort to me." She had no idea how widely that support and comfort would extend, though her awareness of the power in her hands seemed to grow as time passed. One year before her death from typhus in the Bergen-Belsen camp, she wrote, "I want to be useful or give pleasure to people around me who yet don't really know me. I want to go on living even after my death!"

The reason for her immortality is basically literary. She was an extraordinarily good writer, for any age, and the quality of her work seemed a direct result of a ruthlessly honest disposition. Millions were moved by the purified version of her diary originally published by her father, but the recent critical, unexpurgated edition has moved millions more by disanointing her solely as an emblem of innocence. Anne's deep effect on readers comes from her being a normal, if gifted, teenager. She was curious about sex, doubtful about religion, caustic about her parents, irritable especially to herself; she believed she had been fitted with two contradictory souls.

ALL OF THIS HAS MADE HER MORE "USEFUL," IN her terms, as a recognizable human being. She was not simply born blessed with generosity; she struggled toward it by way of self-doubt, impatience, rage, ennui—all things that test the value of a mind. Readers enjoy quoting the diary's sweetest line—"I still believe, in spite of everything, that people are still truly good at heart"—but the passage that follows is more revealing: "I simply can't build up my hopes on a foundation consisting of confusion, misery and death. I see the world gradually being turned into a wilderness; I hear the ever approaching thunder, which will destroy us too; I can feel the sufferings of millions; and yet, if I look up into the heavens, I think that it will all come right, that this cruelty will end, and that peace and tranquillity will return again ... I must uphold my ideals, for perhaps the time will come when I shall be able to carry them out."

Here is no childish optimism but rather a declaration of principles, a way of dealing practically with a world bent on destroying her. It is the cry of the Jew in the attic, but it is also the cry of the 20th century mind, of the refugee forced to wander in deserts of someone else's manufacture, of the invisible man who asserts his visibility. And the telling thing about her statement of "I am" is that it bears no traces of self-indulgence. In a late entry, she wondered, "Is it really good to follow almost entirely my own conscience?" In our time of holy self-expression, the idea that truth lies outside one's own troubles comes close to heresy, yet most people acknowledge its deep validity and admire the girl for it.

Indeed, they love her, which is to say they love the book. Her diary showed the world not only how fine a person she was, but also how necessary it is to come to terms with one's own moral being, even—perhaps especially—when the context is horror. The diary suggests that the story of oneself is all that we have, and that it is worth a life to get it right.

It was interesting that the Franks' secret annex was concealed by a bookcase that swung away from an opening where steps led up to a hidden door. For a while, Anne was protected by books, and then the Nazis pushed them aside to get at a young girl. First you kill the books; then you kill the children. What they could not know is that she had already escaped. ∎

The essayist Roger Rosenblatt is editor at large of Time Inc. He is the author of Children of War.

Helen Keller

Stricken blind and deaf at an early age, she altered our perception of the disabled and remapped the boundaries of the senses

By **DIANE SCHUUR** with **DAVID JACKSON**

HELEN KELLER WAS LESS THAN TWO YEARS OLD when she came down with a fever. It struck dramatically and left her unconscious. The fever went just as suddenly. But she was blinded and, very soon after, deaf. As she grew up, she managed to learn to do tiny errands, but she also realized she was missing something. "Sometimes," she later wrote, "I stood between two persons who were conversing and touched their lips. I could not understand, and was vexed. I moved my lips and gesticulated frantically without result. This made me so angry at times that I kicked and screamed until I was exhausted." She was a wild child.

I can understand her rage. I was born two months prematurely and was placed in an incubator. The practice at the time was to pump a large amount of oxygen into the incubator, something doctors have since learned to be extremely cautious about. As a result, I lost my sight. I was sent to a state school for the blind, but I flunked first grade because Braille just didn't make any sense to me. Words were a weird concept. I remember being hit and slapped. And you act all that in. All rage is anger that is acted in, bottled in for so long that it just pops out. Helen had it harder. She was both blind and deaf. But, oh, the transformation that came over her when she discovered that words were related to things! It's like the lyrics of that song: "On a clear day, rise and look around you, and you'll see who you are."

I can say the word see. I can speak the language of the sighted. That's part of the first great achievement of Helen Keller. She proved how language could liberate the blind and the deaf. She wrote, "Literature is my utopia. Here I am not disenfranchised." But how she struggled to master language. In her book *Midstream*, she wrote about how she was frustrated by the alphabet, by the language of the deaf, even with the speed with which her teacher spelled things out for her on her palm. She was impatient and hungry for words, and her teacher's scribbling on her hand would never be as fast, she thought, as the people who could read the words with their eyes. I remember how books got me going after I finally grasped Braille. Being in that school was like being in an orphanage. But words—and in my case, music—changed that isolation. With language, Keller, who could not hear and could not see, proved she could communicate

With her hand, Keller demonstrates how she can "hear" Anne Sullivan speak

BORN June 27 in Tuscumbia, Ala.	**1887** Anne Sullivan becomes Keller's tutor	**1903** *The Story of My Life* is published	**1919** Begins four-year stretch appearing with Sullivan in vaudeville shows	**1959** *The Miracle Worker* airs on television. It is later adapted for the stage and film

1880 — — — **1968**

1882 At 19 months old, has a high fever and becomes deaf and blind

STUDENT Keller graduates from Radcliffe in 1904

1936 Sullivan dies

1958 *Teacher,* her memoir of Sullivan, is published

DIES June 1 in Westport, Conn.

> **I am deeply interested in politics. I like to have the papers read to me, and I try to understand the great questions of the day.**
>
> HELEN KELLER, in a 1901 letter to Senator George Frisbie Hoar

Celebrities of the day: Keller with Alexander Graham Bell

With Patty Duke, who portrayed her in *The Miracle Worker*

in the world of sight and sound—and was able to speak to it and live in it. I am a beneficiary of her work. Because of her example, the world has given way a little. In my case, I was able to go from the state school for the blind to regular public school from age 11 until my senior year in high school. And then I decided on my own to go back into the school for the blind. Now I sing jazz.

As miraculous as learning language may seem, that achievement of Keller's belongs to the 19th century. It was also a co-production with her persevering teacher, Anne Sullivan. Helen Keller's greater achievement came after Sullivan, her companion and protector, died in 1936. Keller would live 32 more years and in that time would prove that the disabled can be independent. I hate the word handicapped. Keller would too. We are people with inconveniences. We're not charity cases. Asked how disabled veterans of World War II should be treated, she said they would "not want to be treated as heroes. They want to be able to live naturally and to be treated as human beings."

Those people whose only experience of her is *The Miracle Worker* will be surprised to discover her many dimensions. "My work for the blind," she wrote, "has never occupied a center in my personality. My sympathies are with all who struggle for justice." She was a tireless activist for racial and sexual equality. She once said, "I think God made woman foolish so that she might be a suitable companion to man." She had such left-leaning opinions that the FBI under J. Edgar Hoover kept a file on her. And who were her choices for the most important people of the century? Thomas Edison, Charlie Chaplin and Lenin. Furthermore, she did not think appearing on the vaudeville circuit, showing off her skills, was beneath her, even as her friends were shocked that she would venture onto the vulgar stage. She was complex. Her main message was and is, "We're like everybody else. We're here to be able to live a life as full as any sighted person's. And it's O.K. to be ourselves."

That means we have the freedom to be as extraordinary as the sighted. Keller loved an audience and wrote that she adored "the warm tide of human life pulsing round and round me." That's why the stage appealed to her, why she learned to speak and to deliver speeches. And to feel the vibrations of music, of the radio, of the movement of lips. You must understand that even more than sighted people, we need to be touched. When you look at a person, eye to eye, I imagine it's like touching them. We don't have that convenience. But when I perform, I get that experience from a crowd. Helen Keller must have as well. She was our first star. And I am very grateful to her. ∎

Diane Schuur's latest jazz release is Music Is My Life, *available from Atlantic Records.*

Mother Teresa

In fighting for the dignity of the destitute, she gave the world a moral example that bridged divides

By BHARATI MUKHERJEE

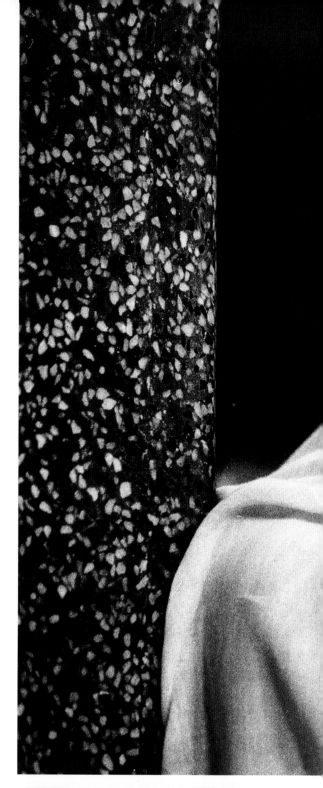

THE BENGALI CHAUVINIST IN ME GOT A THRILL: "THIS IS Peter Jennings, tonight live from Calcutta." For the first and only time in my life, the great city I was born and raised in had hit the big time. Bengalis love to celebrate their language, their culture, their politics, their fierce attachment to a city that has been famously "dying" for more than a century. They resent with equal ferocity the reflex stereotyping that labels any civic dysfunction anywhere in the world "another Calcutta." And why were the American media in Calcutta? For the funeral of an 87-year-old Albanian immigrant by the name of Agnes Gonxha Bojaxhiu.

In this era of "ethnic cleansing," identity politics and dislocation of communities, it is heartening that one of the most marginalized people in recent history—a minority Albanian inside Slavic Macedonia, a minority Roman Catholic among Muslims and Orthodox Christians—should find a home, citizenship and acceptance in an Indian city of countless non-Christians. She blurred the line between insider and outsider that so many today are trying to deepen.

Bojaxhiu was born of Roman Catholic Albanian parents in 1910 in Shkup (now Skopje), a town that straddled the ethnic, linguistic, religious and geological fault line in the then Turkish province, later Yugoslav republic, now absurdly unpronounceable independent state of FYROM (the Former Yugoslav Republic of Macedonia). When she was seven, her father was murdered. Bojaxhiu chose emigration over political activism and at the age of 18 entered the Sisters of Loreto's convent in Ireland as a novice. The teaching order sent her to Bengal in 1929. She spoke broken English and had yet to take her first vows.

I first saw Mother Teresa in the summer of 1951, when I started school at Loreto House in Calcutta. The school was run by the Sisters of Loreto according to directives sent from its principal convent in Ireland. During the British raj, Loreto House had admitted very few Indians. By the time I became a student there, the majority of students were Hindu Bengalis, the daughters of Calcutta's élite families, but the majority of teachers continued to be Irish-born nuns. Mother Teresa was no longer affiliated with the Sisters of Loreto, but she came around

Opposed to abortion, she treasured unwanted babies

BORN Aug. 27, in Shkup, Ottoman Empire

1928 Joins Irish convent

1931 Begins teaching at a Calcutta girls' school

1950 The Pope officially sanctions her order, the Missionaries of Charity

1979 Wins Nobel Peace Prize

1910

1997

1929 Sent to novitiate in Darjeeling, India

1946 Receives "call" to live and work among the poor

1963 Awarded India's Padmashri, for services to the people of India

DIES Sept. 5 in Calcutta

" In the West there is loneliness, which I call the leprosy of the West. In many ways it is worse than our poor in Calcutta. "

MOTHER TERESA

"I have never refused a child," Mother Teresa once said. "Never. Not one"

to our campus every now and then. She had left teaching at another of the Sisters' schools three years before in order to, as she put it, "follow Christ into the slums." The break, as far as we schoolgirls could tell, had not been totally amicable, at least not on the part of the Loreto nuns.

The picture of Mother Teresa that I remember from my childhood is of a short, sari-wearing woman scurrying down a red gravel path between manicured lawns, one or two slower-footed, sari-clad young Indian nuns in tow. We thought her a freak. Probably we'd picked up on unvoiced opinions of our Loreto nuns. We weren't quite sure what an Albanian was except that she wasn't as fully European as our Irish nuns. Or perhaps she seemed odd to us because we had never encountered a nun who wore a sari. The government had made antimissionary noises but hadn't yet cracked down on missionaries' visa applications.

In the early '50s, we non-Christian students at Loreto House were suspicious of Mother Teresa's motives in help-

ing street children and orphans. Was she rescuing these children to convert them? Her antiabortion campaigns among homeless women were as easy for us to ignore as were the antiabortion lectures our nuns delivered twice weekly. Her apparent dread of mortality and her obsession with dignified dying were at odds with Hindu concepts of reincarnation and death as a hoped-for release from maya, the illusory reality of worldly existence.

It wasn't until she set up a leprosarium outside Calcutta on land provided by the government that I began to see her as an idealist rather than an eccentric. Lepers were a common sight all over India and in every part of Calcutta, but extending help beyond dropping a coin or two onto their rag-wrapped stumps was not. The ultimate terror the city held had nothing to do with violence. It was fear of the Other, the poor, the dying—or to evoke a word with biblical authority—the pestilential. And so I could no longer be cynical about her motives. She wasn't just another Christian proselytizer. Her care of lepers changed the mind of many Calcuttans. Young physicians, one the uncle of a classmate, began to sign up as volunteers. It all made Mother Teresa seem less remote. The very people whom she had deserted when she broke with the Loreto nuns were now seeking her out.

I left Calcutta as a teenager and did not return to live there for any length of time until 1973. The Calcutta I went back to was vociferously in love with Mother Teresa. The women I had been close to in Loreto House, women who in the '70s had become socialite wives and volunteer social workers, were devoted to Mother Teresa and her projects, especially the leprosarium. Years later, I learned that the volunteer Mother Teresa had come to rely on was a Loreto House graduate.

It is the fate of moral crusaders to be vulnerable to charges of hypocrisy or have the arbitrary selectiveness of their campaigns held against them. Mother Teresa's detractors have accused her of overemphasizing Calcuttans' destitution and of coercing conversion from the defenseless. In the context of lost causes, Mother Teresa took on battles she knew she could win. Taken together, it seems to me, the criticisms of her work do not undermine or topple her overall achievement. The real test might be, Did she inspire followers, skeptics and even opponents to larger acts of kindness or greater visions of possibility? If the church demands hard evidence of a miracle for sainthood, the transformation of many hearts might make the strongest case. ∎

Bharati Mukherjee's novels include Jasmine, The Holder of the World *and* Leave It to Me.

Four Saints For All Seasons

In a century dominated by materialism, capitalism and science, these souls dared to advocate the spiritual life

Dalai Lama

The avatar of the Bodhisattva Avalokiteshvara, he is the spiritual and temporal ruler of Tibetan Buddhists—and thus the bulwark of the struggle against China's continuing occupation of his homeland.

Padre Pio

The miracle-working Italian monk exhibited stigmata and was credited with healing. It was said he could be in two places at once. He is up for canonization.

Mother Hale

Clara Hale always said, "I'm simply a person who loves children." And she proved it: her Hale House took in and cared for hundreds of babies abandoned in New York City's drug and AIDS epidemics.

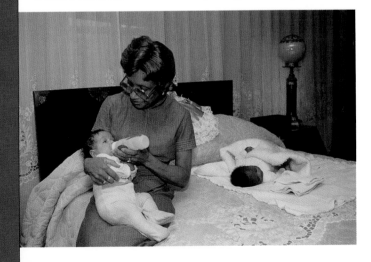

Krishnamurti

In 1909, as a teenager, he was proclaimed an incarnation of the Buddha, or World Teacher. He later repudiated these messianic claims and spent his life enunciating and exemplifying a secular approach to Asian mysticism.

Muhammad Ali

Floating, stinging, punching, prophesying, he transformed his sport and became the world's most adored athlete

By **GEORGE PLIMPTON**

OLIVER WENDELL HOLMES ONCE OBSERVED THAT every profession is great that is greatly pursued. Boxing in the early '60s, largely controlled by the Mob, was in a moribund state until Muhammad Ali—Cassius Clay, in those days—came on the scene. "Just when the sweet science appears to lie like a painted ship upon a painted ocean," wrote A.J. Liebling, "a new Hero ... comes along like a Moran tug to pull it out of the ocean."

Though Ali won the gold medal at the Rome Olympics in 1960, at the time the experts didn't think much of his boxing skills. His head, eyes wide, seemed to float above the action. Rather than slip a punch, the traditional defensive move, it was his habit to sway back, bending at the waist—a tactic that appalled the experts. Lunacy.

The King vs. the Greatest? We're betting on the guy at right

Nor did they approve of his personal behavior: the self-promotions ("I am the greatest!"), his affiliation with the Nation of Islam and giving up his "slave name" for Muhammad Ali ("I don't have to be what you want me to be; I'm free to be what I want"), the poetry (his ability to compose rhymes on the run could very well qualify him as the first rapper) or the quips ("If Ali says a mosquito can pull a plow, don't ask how. Hitch him up!"). At the press conferences, the reporters were sullen. Ali would turn on them. "Why ain't you taking notice?" or "Why ain't you laughing?"

It was odd that they weren't. He was an engaging combination of sass and sweetness and naiveté. His girlfriend disclosed that the first time he was kissed, he fainted. Merriment always seemed to be bubbling just below the surface, even when the topic was somber. When reporters asked about his affiliation with Islam, he joked that he was going to have four wives: one to shine his shoes, one to feed him grapes, one to rub oil on his muscles and one named Peaches. In his boyhood he was ever the prankster and the practical joker. His idea of fun was to frighten his parents—putting a sheet over his head and jumping out at them from a closet, or tying a string to a bedroom curtain

BORN Cassius Clay, Jan. 17, in Louisville, Ky.	1960 Wins an Olympic gold medal	1974 Defeats George Foreman in the "Rumble in the Jungle" in Zaïre	1981 Retires from boxing	
1942				
	1964 Wins heavyweight title from Sonny Liston; becomes Muhammad Ali	1975 Defeats Joe Frazier in the "Thrilla in Manila" in the Philippines		1996 Opens the Olympic Games in Atlanta

1996 Opens the Olympic Games in Atlanta

> ❝ I'm not only the greatest; I'm the double greatest.
> Not only do I knock 'em out, I pick the round. ❞
>
> **MUHAMMAD ALI, in 1962 to the New York *Times***

Ali deeply respected Black Muslim leader Elijah Muhammad

and then making it move after his parents had gone to bed.

The public as well had a hard time accepting him. His fight for the heavyweight championship in Miami against Sonny Liston was sparsely attended. Indeed, public sentiment was counting on Liston, a Mob-controlled thug, to take care of the lippy upstart. Liston concurred, saying he was going to put his fist so far down his opponent's throat, he was going to have trouble removing it.

Then, of course, three years after Ali defended the championship, there came the public vilification for his refusal to join the Army during the Vietnam War—"I ain't got no quarrel with them Viet Cong"—one of the more telling remarks of the era. The government prosecuted him for draft dodging, and the boxing commissions took away his license. He was idle for 3½ years at the peak of his career. In 1971 the Supreme Court ruled that the government had acted improperly. But Ali bore the commissions no ill will.

There were no lawsuits to get his title back through the courts. No need, he said, to punish them for doing what they thought was right. Quite properly, in his mind, he won back the title in the ring, knocking out George Foreman in the eighth round of their fight in Zaïre—the "Rumble in the Jungle."

Ali was asked on a TV show what he would have done with his life, given a choice. After an awkward pause—a rare thing, indeed—he admitted he couldn't think of anything other than boxing. That is all he had ever wanted or wished for. He defended boxing as a sport: "You don't have to be hit in boxing. People don't understand that."

He was wrong. Joe Frazier said he had hit Ali with punches that would have brought down a building. Coaxed into fights by his managers long after he should have retired, and perhaps because he loved the sport too much to leave it, Ali ended up being punished by the likes of Leon Spinks and Larry Holmes, who took little pleasure in what they were doing.

Oscar Wilde once suggested that you kill the thing you love. In Ali's case, it was the reverse: what he loved, in a sense, killed him. The man who was the most loquacious of athletes ("I am the onliest of boxing's poet laureates") now says almost nothing: he moves slowly through the crowds and signs auto-

Ali (and his big mouth) earned more than all previous heavyweight champs combined

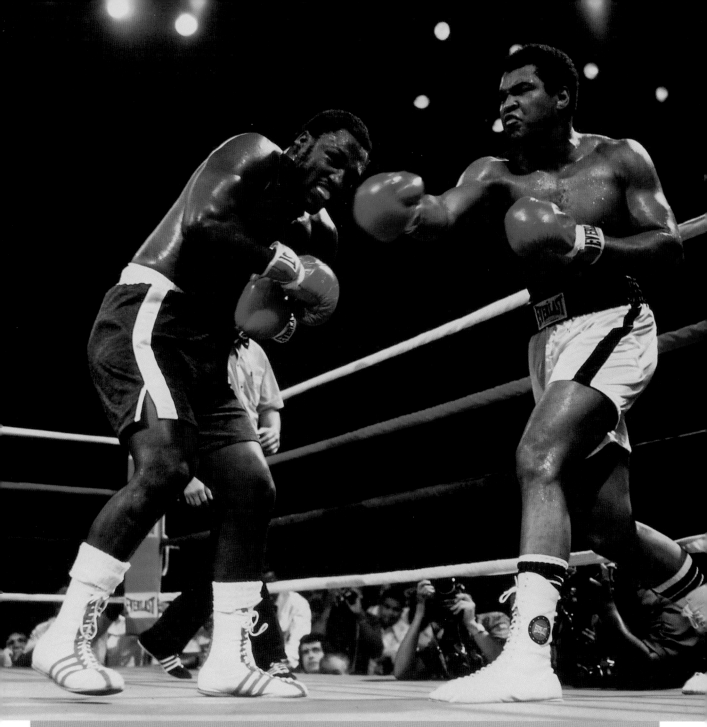

Asked to name his toughest fight, Ali chose the 1975 "Thrilla in Manila," when he outlasted Joe Frazier in a brutal slugfest

graphs. He has probably signed more autographs than any other athlete ever. It is his principal activity at home, working at his desk. He was once denied an autograph by his idol, Sugar Ray Robinson, and vowed he would never turn anyone down. The volume of mail is enormous.

The ceremonial leave-taking of great athletes can impart indelible memories, even if one remembers them from the scratchy newsreels of time—Babe Ruth with the doffed cap at home plate, Lou Gehrig's voice echoing in the vast hollows of Yankee Stadium. Muhammad Ali's was not exactly a leave-taking, but it may have seemed so to the estimated 3 billion television viewers who saw him open the Atlanta Olympics in 1996. Outfitted in a white gym suit that eerily made him seem to glisten against a dark night sky, he approached the unlit saucer with his flaming torch, his free arm trembling visibly from the effects of Parkinson's.

It was a kind of epiphany: those who watched realized how much they missed him and how much he had contributed to the world of sport. Students of boxing will pore over the trio of Ali-Frazier fights, which rank among the greatest in fistic history, as one might read three acts of a great drama. They would remember the shenanigans, the Ali Shuffle, the Rope-a-Dope, the fact that Ali had brought beauty and grace to the most uncompromising of sports. And they would marvel that through the wonderful excesses of skill and character, he had become the most famous athlete, indeed, the best-known personage in the world. ∎

George Plimpton, editor of the Paris Review, *is the author of* Truman Capote *and a number of books on sport.*

The Century's 10 Most Influential Athletes

As sport became entertainment, these innovators shaped the modern game

Babe Ruth

In sports' first golden age, there was Babe Ruth—and then there was everyone else. His assault on distant fences bent baseball into a new and thrilling shape. His appetites were as prodigious as his home runs, his affinity for the crowd and the camera a part of his DNA.

Jacques Plante

When he affixed a piece of molded fiberglass to his head in 1959, he was able to venture out from his circumscribed piece of ice in front of the Montreal net. After him, goalies displayed a new daring, a more aggressive posture—and more teeth.

Bobby Jones

The embodiment of the sportsman, he won an unprecedented (and still unmatched) 13 major championships in a brief seven years, then retired at 28 to found the Masters Tournament on his Augusta National course.

Secretariat

In 1973 the big chestnut colt won the first Triple Crown in 25 years by 31 incredible lengths. In appearance, style and heart he was the Platonic ideal, the standard against which all Thoroughbreds must be measured..

Jesse Owens

For one brief shining moment, he was white America's first black athletic hero, his four gold medals (and three world records) at the 1936 Berlin Olympics a garland of honor for the U.S., a rebuke to Hitler and a beacon to black Americans.

Curt Flood

When the St. Louis Cards' outfielder sued baseball in 1970 to win the right to sell his services to the highest bidder, he initiated a process that would destroy the feudal structure of pro sports. He lost his battle, but his fellow players, in time, won the war.

Vince Lombardi

He was the essence of coach, this gruff, gap-toothed tyrant-with-a-heart-of-gold who engineered championships—five in seven seasons—not from brilliant constellations of X's and O's but from his total commitment to the idea of a team.

Johnny Unitas

In the NFL's coming-out party, he led his Baltimore Colts to a 23-17 overtime victory over the New York Giants in the 1958 championship game. He was the first of the modern quarterbacks in a sport they have dominated every since.

Michael Jordan

Magic Johnson: "When you talk about beautiful basketball, the way Mr. Naismith drew it up to be played, you're talking about Michael Jordan." Shaquille O'Neal: "I'll tell my grandchildren I got to play against him." 'Nuff said?

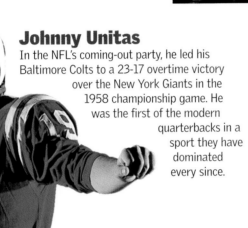

Billie Jean King

Before Martina and Steffi, there was Billie Jean Moffitt King, 20 times a Wimbledon champion. She changed the way we look at female athletes—and the way they look at one another. "She was a crusader fighting a battle for all of us," said Navratilova.

Jackie
Robinson

He stole fans' hearts with his speed and daring, and by shattering baseball's color barrier, he changed the face of the nation forever

By HENRY AARON

I WAS 14 YEARS OLD WHEN I FIRST SAW JACKIE ROBINSON. It was the spring of 1948, the year after Jackie changed my life by breaking baseball's color line. His team, the Brooklyn Dodgers, made a stop in my hometown of Mobile, Ala., while barnstorming its way north to start the season, and while he was there, Jackie spoke to a big crowd of black folks over on Davis Avenue. I think he talked about segregation, but I didn't hear a word that came out of his mouth. Jackie Robinson was such a hero to me that I couldn't do anything but gawk at him.

They say certain people are bigger than life, but Jackie Robinson is the only man I've known who truly was. In 1947 life in America—at least my America, and Jackie's—was segregation. It was two worlds that were afraid of each other. There were separate schools for blacks and whites, separate restaurants, separate hotels, separate drinking fountains and separate baseball leagues. Life was unkind to black people who tried to bring those worlds together. It could be hateful. But Jackie Robinson, God bless him, was bigger than all of that.

Jackie Robinson had to be bigger than life. He had to be bigger than the Brooklyn teammates who got up a petition to keep him off the ball club, bigger than the pitchers who threw at him or the base runners who dug their spikes into his shin, bigger than the bench jockeys who hollered for him to carry their bags and shine their shoes, bigger than the so-called fans who wrote him death threats.

When Branch Rickey first met with Jackie about joining the Dodgers, he told him that for three years he would have to turn the other cheek and silently suffer all the vile things that would come his way. Believe me, it wasn't Jackie's nature to do that. He was a fighter, the proudest and most competitive person I've ever seen. This was a man who, as a lieutenant in the Army, risked a court-martial by refusing to sit in the back of a military bus. But when Rickey read to him from *The Life of Christ*, Jackie understood the wisdom and the necessity of forbearance.

To this day, I don't know how he withstood the things he did without lashing back. I've been through a lot in my time, and I consider myself to be a patient man, but I know I couldn't have done what Jackie did. I don't think anybody else could have done it. Somehow, though, Jackie had the strength to suppress his instincts, to sacrifice his pride for his people's. It was an incredible act of selflessness that brought the races closer together than ever before and shaped the dreams of an entire generation.

Before Jackie Robinson broke the color line, I wasn't permitted even to think about being a professional baseball player. I once mentioned something to my father about it, and he said, "Ain't no colored ballplayers." There were the Negro Leagues, of course, where the Dodgers discovered Jackie, but my mother, like most, would rather her son be a schoolteacher than a Negro Leaguer. All that changed when Jackie started stealing bases in a Brooklyn uniform.

Jackie's character was much more important than his batting average, but it certainly helped that he was a great

BORN Jan. 31 in Cairo, Ga.

1945 Joins Kansas City Monarchs of Negro League, then the Dodgers' farm team in Montreal

1949 Wins National League's Most Valuable Player award

1962 Inducted into Hall of Fame

1919

1972

ROBINSON was the first athlete in the history of UCLA to win letters in four sports

1939 Enrolls at UCLA; stars in football and track

1942 Enlists in the U.S. Army

1947 Begins playing for the Dodgers

1956 Plays final season

DIED Oct. 24 in Stamford, Conn.

" By walking among them and showing everyone we could keep our heads high, he helped bring our whole society together. "

FRANK ROBINSON, the first black manager of a major league team

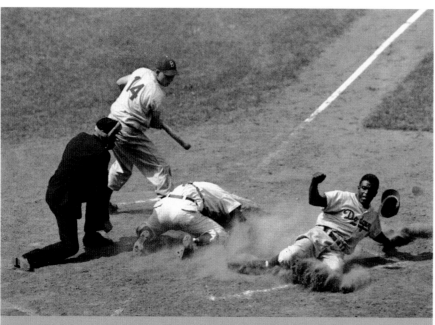

Robinson slides home in 1947—one of the speedster's record 19 steals of home plate

Gibson and others—dominated the National League. If we played as if we were on a mission, it was because Jackie Robinson had sent us out on one.

Even after he retired in 1956 and was inducted into the Hall of Fame in 1962, Jackie continued to chop along the path that was still a long way from being cleared. He campaigned for baseball to hire a black third-base coach, then a black manager. In 1969 he refused an invitation to play in an old-timers' game at Yankee Stadium to protest the lack of progress along those lines.

A great star from my generation, Frank Robinson (who was related to Jackie only in spirit), finally became the first black manager, in 1975. Jackie was gone by then. His last public appearance was at the 1972 World Series; he showed up with white hair, carrying a cane and going blind from diabetes. He died nine days later.

ballplayer, a .311 career hitter whose trademark was rattling pitchers and fielders with his daring base running. He wasn't the best Negro League talent at the time he was chosen, and baseball wasn't really his best sport—he had been a football and track star at UCLA—but he played the game with a ferocious creativity that gave the country a good idea of what it had been missing all those years. With Jackie in the infield, the Dodgers won six National League pennants.

I believe every black person in America had a piece of those pennants. There's never been another ballplayer who touched people as Jackie did. The only comparable athlete, in my experience, was Joe Louis. The difference was that Louis competed against white men; Jackie competed with them as well. He was taking us over segregation's threshold into a new land whose scenery made every black person stop and stare in reverence. We were all with Jackie. We slid into every base that he swiped, ducked at every fastball that hurtled toward his head. The circulation of the Pittsburgh *Courier,* the leading black newspaper, increased by 100,000 when it began reporting on him regularly. All over the country, black preachers would call together their congregations just to pray for Jackie and urge them to demonstrate the same forbearance that he did.

Later in his career, when the "Great Experiment" had proved to be successful, Jackie allowed his instincts to take over in issues of race. He began striking back and speaking out. And when Jackie Robinson spoke, every black player got the message. He made it clear to us that we weren't playing just for ourselves or for our teams; we were playing for our people. I don't think it's a coincidence that the black players of the late '50s and '60s—me, Roy Campanella, Monte Irvin, Willie Mays, Ernie Banks, Frank Robinson, Bob

Most of the black players from Jackie's day were at the funeral, but I was appalled by how few of the younger players showed up to pay him tribute. At the time, I was 41 home runs short of Babe Ruth's career record, and I felt that it was up to me to keep Jackie's dream alive. I was inspired to dedicate my home-run record to the same great cause to which he dedicated his life. I'm still inspired by Jackie Robinson. Hardly a day goes by that I don't think of him. ∎

Henry ("Hank") Aaron holds the major league career home-run record (755) and works for the Atlanta Braves organization.

With his family; off the field, Robinson cherished his privacy

Women in Sports: Four Pacesetters

Leading the fast break to equality, they proved a woman's place was on the field, the court and the tee

Martina Navratilova

The Czech defector infused women's tennis with raw physical power, winning 167 singles titles, 18 of them Grand Slams. As America's first major athlete to be openly gay, she lost endorsements— but opened doors for others.

Althea Gibson

She discovered tennis while in the custody of New York City's welfare department. Venturing where no African American had gone before, she won Wimbledon and the U.S. Open championship in 1957 and 1958, paving the way for such stars as Arthur Ashe, Sheryl Swoopes and Tiger Woods.

Mildred Didrikson

"The Babe," nicknamed for her killer baseball swing, was arguably the best all-around athlete of the century—even if she was a girl. Before winning 55 golf tournaments, the defiantly unfrilly jock took on basketball (a three-time All-American), track (two gold medals at the 1932 Olympics), bowling and billiards.

Mia Hamm

The relentless, high-scoring forward sparked "Mia-mania" among teenage girls when she led the U.S. women's team to victory in soccer's 1999 World Cup. Always a reluctant diva, Hamm was the epitome of the team player.

Apotheosis: After his final game in 1977, in which Pelé played one half with the New York Cosmos and the other with a team of Brazilian all-stars

Pelé

He dominated soccer for two decades with a passion matched only by that of his worldwide gallery of fans

By HENRY KISSINGER

HEROES WALK ALONE, BUT THEY BECOME MYTHS when they ennoble the lives and touch the hearts of all of us. For those millions of fans worldwide who love soccer, Edson Arantes do Nascimento, generally known as Pelé, is a hero.

Performance at a high level in any sport is to exceed the ordinary human scale. But Pelé's performance transcended that of the ordinary star by as much as the star exceeds ordinary performance. He scored an average of a goal in every international game he played—the equivalent of a baseball player's hitting a home run in every World Series game over 15 years. Between 1956 and 1974, Pelé scored a total of 1,220 goals—not unlike hitting an average of 70 home runs every year for a decade and a half.

While he played, his Brazil team won the World Cup, staged quadrennially, three times in 12 years. He scored five goals in a game six times, four goals 30 times and three goals 90 times. And he did so not aloofly or disdainfully—as do many modern stars—but with an infectious joy that caused even the teams over which he triumphed to share in his pleasure, for it is no disgrace to be defeated by a phenomenon defying emulation.

He was born across the mountains from the great coastal cities of Brazil, in the impoverished town of Tres Corações. Nicknamed Dico by his family, he was called Pelé by soccer friends, a word whose origins escape him. Dico shined shoes until he was discovered at the age of 11 by one of the country's premier players, Waldemar de Brito. Four years later, Brito brought Pelé to São Paulo and declared to the disbelieving directors of the professional team in Santos, "This boy will be the greatest soccer player in the world." He was quickly legend. By the next season, he was the top scorer in his league. As the *Times* of London would later say, "How do you spell Pelé? G-O-D." He has been known to stop war: both sides in Nigeria's civil war called a 48-hour cease-fire in 1967 so Pelé could play an exhibition match in Lagos.

To understand Pelé's role in soccer, some discussion of the nature of the game is necessary. No team sport evokes the same sort of primal, universal passion as soccer. During the World Cup, the matches of the national football teams impose television schedules on the rhythm of life. In 1998 I attended a dinner for leading members of the British establishment and distinguished guests from all over the world in London. The hosts had the bad luck to have chosen the night of the match between England and Argentina—always a blood feud, compounded on this occasion by the memory of the Falklands crisis. The impeccable audience insisted that television sets be set up at strategic locations, during both the reception and the dinner. The match went into overtime, so the main speaker did not get to deliver his message until 11 p.m. And since England lost, many listeners were not precisely in a mood for anything but mourning.

When France finally won that World Cup, Paris was paralyzed with joy for nearly 48 hours, Brazil by dejection for a similar period. I was in Brazil in 1962 when the national

BORN Oct. 23 in Tres Corações, in the Brazilian state of Minas Gerais

1958 In his first World Cup appearance, leads Brazil to victory

1974 Signals he'll retire by picking up the ball 20 minutes into game and kneeling in midfield

1977 Retires from Cosmos

1994 Long at odds with FIFA, the world soccer authority, he is named Brazil's Minister of Sports

1940

1956 Begins pro career with Santos Football Club, which wins nine championships between 1958 and 1969

1975 In financial trouble, comes out of retirement to play for New York Cosmos

1970 Scoring in the World Cup final game: Brazil won

I was screaming Gooooaaaaalllll!!!! … running and jumping in the air with a release of unbearable tension.

PELE, on scoring in his first World Cup in 1958

The soaring star shows off his grace and athleticism with a bicycle kick against Belgium in 1964

team won the World Cup in Chile. Everything stopped for two days while Rio celebrated a premature carnival.

There is no comparable phenomenon in the U.S. Our fans do not identify with their teams in such a way partly because American team sports are more cerebral and require a degree of skill that is beyond the reach of the layman. Baseball, for instance, requires a bundle of disparate skills: hitting a ball thrown at 90 m.p.h., catching a ball flying at the speed of a bullet, and throwing long distances with great accuracy. Football requires a different set of skills for each of its 11 positions. The U.S. spectator thus finds himself viewing two discrete events: what is actually taking place on the playing field and the translation of it into detailed and minute statistics. He wants his team to win, but he is also committed to the statistical triumph of the star he admires. The American sports hero is like Joe DiMaggio—a kind of Lone Ranger who walks in solitude beyond the reach of common experience, lifting us beyond ourselves.

Soccer is an altogether different sort of game. All 11 players must possess the same type of skills—especially in modern soccer, where the distinction between offensive and defensive players has dissolved. Being continuous, the game does not lend itself to being broken down into a series of component plays that, as in football or baseball, can be practiced. Baseball and football thrill by the perfection of their repetitions, soccer by the improvisation of solutions to ever changing strategic necessities. Soccer requires little equipment, other than a pair of shoes. Everybody believes he can play soccer. And it can be played by any number of players

as a pickup game. Thus soccer outside North America is truly a game for the masses, which can identify with its passions, its sudden triumphs and its inevitable disillusionments. Baseball and football are an exaltation of the human experience; soccer is its incarnation.

Pelé is therefore a different phenomenon from the baseball or football star. Soccer stars are dependent on their teams even while transcending them. To achieve mythic status as a soccer player is especially difficult because only the fewest players perform at the top of their game for more than five years. Incredibly, Pelé performed at the highest level for 18 years, scoring 52 goals in 1973, his 17th year. Contemporary soccer superstars never reach even 50 goals a season. For Pelé, who had thrice scored more than 100 goals a year, it signaled retirement.

THE MYTHIC STATUS OF PELE DERIVES AS WELL FROM the way he incarnated the character of Brazil's national team. Its style affirms that virtue without joy is a contradiction in terms. Its players are the most acrobatic, if not always the most proficient. Brazilian teams play with a contagious exuberance. When those yellow shirts go on the attack—which is most of the time—and their fans cheer to the intoxicating beat of samba bands, soccer becomes a ritual of fluidity and grace. In Pelé's heyday, the Brazilians epitomized soccer as fantasy.

I saw Pelé at his peak only once, at the final of the World Cup in 1970. Opponent Italy played its tough defense coupled with sudden thrusts to tie the game 1-1, demoralizing the Brazilians. Italy could very easily have massed its defense even more, forcing its frantic opponents to make the mistakes that would encompass their ruin. But, led by Pelé, Brazil refused to quit. Attacking as if the Italians were a practice team, the Brazilians ran them into the ground, 4-1.

I saw Pelé play for the New York Cosmos a few times: he was no longer as fast, but he was as exuberant as ever. By then, he was an institution. Most modern fans never saw him play, yet they somehow feel he is part of their lives. He made the transition from superstar to mythic figure. ∎

Henry Kissinger, former Secretary of State, was instrumental in bringing World Cup soccer to the U.S. in 1994.

Bruce Lee

With nothing but his hands (a.k.a. fists of fury), feet and a
whole lot of attitude, he turned the little guy into a tough guy

By JOEL STEIN

"[Lee had] intense personal magnetism: even when he was just walking, the Dragon seemed to crackle with electricity"

JACKIE CHAN, who was a young stuntman in Lee's films

Looking to show off his physique, the young Lee trademarked a sinewy, threatening pose

NOT A GOOD CENTURY FOR THE CHINESE. AFTER dominating much of the past two millenniums in science and philosophy, they've spent the past 100 years being invaded, split apart and patronizingly lectured by the West. And, let's face it, this communism thing isn't working out either.

But in 1959 a short, skinny, bespectacled 18-year-old kid traveled from Hong Kong to America and declared himself to be John Wayne, James Dean, Charles Atlas and the guy who kicked your butt in junior high. In an America where the Chinese were still stereotyped as meek house servants and railroad workers, Bruce Lee was all steely sinew, threatening stare and cocky, pointed finger—a Clark Kent who didn't need to change outfits. He was the redeemer, not only for the Chinese but for all the geeks and dorks and pimpled teenage masses that washed up at the theaters to see his action movies. He was David, with spin-kicks and flying leaps more captivating than any slingshot.

He is the patron saint of the cult of the body: the almost mystical belief that we have the power to overcome adversity if only we submit to the right combinations of exercise, diet, meditation and weight training; that by force of will, we can sculpt ourselves into demigods. The century began with a crazy burst of that philosophy. In 1900 the Boxer rebels of China who attacked the Western embassies in Beijing thought that martial-arts training made them immune to bullets. It didn't. But a related fanaticism—on this side of sanity—exists today: the belief that the human body can be primed for killer perfection and immortal endurance.

Lee never looked like Arnold Schwarzenegger or achieved immortality. He died at 32 under a cloud of controversy, in his mistress's home, of a brain edema, which an autopsy said was caused by a reaction to a prescription painkiller called Equagesic. At that point, he had starred in only three released movies, one of which was unwatchably bad, the other two of which were watchably bad. Although he was a popular movie star in Asia, his New York *Times* obit ran only eight sentences, one of which read "Vincent Canby, the film critic of the New York *Times,* said that movies like *Fists of Fury* make 'the worst Italian western look like the most solemn and noble achievements of the early Soviet Cinema.'"

What Canby missed is that it's the moments between the plot points that are worth watching. It was the ballet of precision violence that flew off the screen; every combination you can create in *Mortal Kombat* can be found in a Lee movie. No one could make violence as beautiful as Lee's. He had a cockiness that passed for charisma. And when he whooped like a crane, jumped in the air and simultaneously kicked two bad guys into unconsciousness, all while punch-

BORN Nov. 27 in San Francisco

1946 Appears in first of many films as child actor

1959 Moves to San Francisco

1966 Portrays Kato in *Green Hornet* TV series

1971 *Fists of Fury* released

1940

1941 Returns with family to Hong Kong

1953 Loses a street fight and starts kung fu lessons

1963 Opens his first kung fu school

1973

DIED July 20 of brain edema, a month before the premiere of *Enter the Dragon*

ing out two others mostly off-screen, you knew the real Lee could do that too.

He spent his life turning his small body into a large weapon. Born sickly in a San Francisco hospital (his father, a Hong Kong opera singer, was on tour there), he would be burdened with two stigmas that don't become an action hero: an undescended testicle and a female name, Li Jun Fan, which his mother gave him to ward off the evil spirits out to snatch valuable male children. She even had one of his ears pierced, because evil spirits always fall for the pierced-ear trick.

Lee quickly became obsessed with martial arts and body building and not much else. As a child actor back in Hong Kong, Lee appeared in 20 movies and rarely in school. He was part of a small gang that was big enough to cause his mother to ship him to America before his 18th birthday so he could claim his dual citizenship and avoid winding up in jail. Boarding at a family friend's Chinese restaurant in Seattle, Lee got a job teaching the Wing Chun style of martial arts he had learned in Hong Kong. In 1964, at a tournament in Long Beach, Calif.—the first major American demonstration of kung fu—Lee, an unknown, ripped through black belt Dan Inosanto so quickly that Inosanto asked to be his student.

Enter the Dragon became a hit only a month after Lee died

Lee's son Brandon died in 1993 while making his first film

Shortly after, Lee landed his first U.S. show-biz role: Kato in *The Green Hornet*, a 1966-67 TV superhero drama from the creators of *Batman*. With this minor celebrity, he attracted students like Steve McQueen, James Coburn and Kareem Abdul-Jabbar to a martial art he called Jeet Kune Do, "the way of the intercepting fist." Living in L.A., he was in the vanguard of all things '70s. He was a physical-fitness freak: running, lifting weights and experimenting with isometrics and electrical impulses meant to stimulate his muscles while he slept. He took vitamins, ginseng, royal jelly,

steroids and even liquid steaks. A rebel, he flouted the Boxer-era tradition of not teaching kung fu to Westerners even as he railed against the robotic exercises of other martial arts that prevented self-expression. One of his admonitions: "Research your own experiences for the truth. Absorb what is useful ... Add what is specifically your own ... The creating individual ... is more important than any style or system." When he died, doctors found traces of marijuana in his body. They could have saved some money on the autopsy and just read those words.

Despite his readiness to embrace American individuality and culture, Lee couldn't get Hollywood to embrace him, so he returned to Hong Kong to make films. In them, Lee chose to represent the little guy—a very cocky little guy—who'd fight for the Chinese against the invading Japanese or the small-town family against the city-living drug dealers. There were, for some reason, usually about 100 of these enemies, but they mostly died as soon as he punched them in the face. The plots were uniform: Lee makes a vow not to fight; people close to Lee are exploited and killed; Lee kills lots of people to retaliate; Lee turns himself in for punishment.

The films set box-office records in Asia, and so Hollywood finally gave him the American action movie he longed to make. But Lee died a month before the release of his first U.S. film, *Enter the Dragon*. The movie would make more than $200 million, and college kids would pin Lee posters next to Che Guevara's. In the end, Lee could only exist young and in the movies. Briefly, he burst out against greater powers before giving himself over to the authorities. A star turn in a century not good for the Chinese.   ■

Joel Stein is a columnist and staff writer for TIME.

Marilyn
Monroe

She sauntered through life as the most delectable sex symbol of the century and became its most enduring pop confection

By PAUL RUDNICK

HOW MUCH DECONSTRUCTION CAN ONE BLOND BEAR? JUST ABOUT everyone has had a go at Marilyn Monroe. There have been more than 300 biographies, learned essays by Steinem and Kael, countless documentaries, drag queens, tattoos, Warhol silk screens and porcelain collector's dolls. Marilyn has gone from actress to icon to licensed brand name; only Elvis and James Dean rival her in market share. At this point, she seems almost beyond comment, like Coca-Cola or Levi's. How did a woman who died a suicide at 36, after starring in only a handful of movies, become such an epic commodity?

Much has been made of Marilyn's desperate personal history, the litany of abusive foster homes and the predatory Hollywood scum who accompanied her wriggle to stardom. Her heavily flashbulbed marriages included bouts with baseball great Joe DiMaggio and literary champ Arthur Miller, and her off-duty trysts involved Sinatra and the rumor of multiple Kennedys. The unauthorized tell-alls burst with miscarriages, abortions, rest cures and frenzied press conferences announcing her desire to be left alone. Her death has been variously attributed to an accidental overdose, political necessity and a Mob hit. Her yummily lurid bio has provided fodder for everything from a failed Broadway musical to Jackie Susann's trash classics to a fictionalized portrait in Miller's play *After the Fall.* Marilyn's media-drenched image as a tragic dumb blond has become an American archetype, along with the Marlboro Man and the Harley-straddling Wild One.

Yet biographical trauma, even when packed with celebrities, cannot account for Marilyn's enduring stature as a goddess and postage stamp. Jacqueline Onassis will be remembered for her timeline, for her participation in events and marriages that mesmerized the planet. Marilyn seems far less factual, more Cinderella or Circe than mortal. There have been other megablonds of varying skills—a pinup parade that includes Jean Harlow, Carole Lombard, Jayne Mansfield and Madonna—so why does Marilyn still seem to have patented the peroxide that they've passed along?

Marilyn may represent some unique alchemy of sex, talent and Technicolor. She is pure movies. I recently watched her as Lorelei Lee in her musical smash, *Gentlemen Prefer Blondes.* The film is an ideal mating of star and role, as Marilyn deliriously embodies author Anita Loos' seminal, shame-free gold digger. Lorelei's honey-voiced, pixilated charm may be best expressed by her line, regarding one of her sugar daddies, "Sometimes Mr. Esmond finds it very difficult to say no to me." Whenever Lorelei appears onscreen, undulating in second-skin, cleavage-proud knitwear or the sheerest orange chiffon,

> ❝ If I'm going to be a symbol of something I'd rather have it sex than some other things we've got symbols of. ❞
>
> **MARILYN MONROE**

In 1954 with second husband Joe DiMaggio at New York's Stork Club

all heads turn, salivate and explode. Who but Marilyn could so effortlessly justify such luscious insanity? She is the absolute triumph of political incorrectness. When she swivels aboard a cruise ship in clinging jersey and a floor-length leopard-skin scarf and matching muff, she handily offends feminists, animal-rights activists and good Christians everywhere—and she wins, because shimmering, jewel-encrusted, heedless movie stardom defeats all common morality.

Marilyn's wit completes her cosmic victory, particularly in her facial expression of painful, soul-wrenching yearning when gazing upon a diamond tiara, a trinket she initially attempts to wear around her neck. Discovering the item's true function, she burbles, "I always love finding new places to wear diamonds!" Movies can offer a very specific bliss, the gorgeousness of a perfectly lighted fairy tale. Watching Marilyn operate her lips and eyebrows while breathlessly seducing an elderly millionaire is like experiencing the invention of ice cream.

Marilyn wasn't quite an actress, in any repertory manner, and she was reportedly an increasing nightmare to work with, recklessly spoiled and unsure, barely able to complete even the briefest scene between breakdowns. Only in the movies can such impossible behavior, and such peculiar, erratic gifts, create eternal magic—only the camera has the mechanical patience to capture the maddening glory of a celluloid savant like Monroe. At her best, playing warmhearted floozies in *Some Like It Hot* and *Bus Stop*, she's like a slightly bruised moonbeam, something fragile and funny and imperiled.

I don't think audiences ever truly identify with Marilyn. They may love her or fear for her, but mostly they simply marvel at her existence, at the delicious unlikeliness of such platinum innocence. She's the bad girl and good girl combined: she's sharp and sexy yet incapable of meanness, a dewy Venus rising from the motel sheets, a hopelessly irresistible home wrecker. Monroe longed to be taken seriously as an artist, but her work in more turgid vehicles, like *The Misfits*, was neither original nor very interesting. She needs the tickle of cashmere to enchant for the ages.

Movies have lent the most perishable qualities, such as youth, beauty and comedy, a millennial shelf life. Until the cameras rolled, stars of the past could only be remembered, not experienced. Had she been born earlier, Marilyn might have existed as only a legendary rumor, a Helen of Troy or

BORN Norma Jeane Baker on June 1 in Los Angeles

DARK DAYS When she was Norma Jeane: the famous blond in her brunet period

1946 Changes name to Marilyn Monroe

1949 Poses for nude calendar shots

1950 Launches career with role in *All About Eve*

1953 *Gentlemen Prefer Blondes*

1954 Weds Joe DiMaggio

1956 Marries Arthur Miller

1959 *Some Like It Hot*

DIES Aug. 5, a suicide

1927

1962

Singing *Diamonds Are a Girl's Best Friend* in *Gentlemen Prefer Blondes*

Tinker Bell. But thanks to Blockbuster, every generation now has immediate access to the evanescent perfection of Marilyn bumping and cooing her way through that chorine's anthem, *Diamonds Are a Girl's Best Friend,* in *Gentlemen Prefer Blondes.* Only movie stars have the chance to live possibly forever, and maybe that's why they're all so crazy. Madonna remade *Diamonds* in the video of her hit *Material Girl,* mimicking Marilyn's hot-pink gown and hot-number choreography, and the sly homage seemed fitting: a blond tribute, a legacy of greedy flirtation. Madonna is too marvelously sane ever to become Marilyn. Madonna's detailed appreciation of fleeting style and the history of sensuality is part of her own arsenal, making her a star and a fan in one. Madonna wisely and affectionately honors the brazen spark in Marilyn, the giddy candy-box allure, and not the easy heartbreak.

Marilyn's tabloid appeal is infinite but ultimately beside the point. Whatever destroyed her—be it Hollywood economics or rabid sexism or her own tormented psyche—pales beside the delight she continues to provide. At her peak, Marilyn was very much like Coca-Cola or Levi's—she was something wonderfully and irrepressibly American. ■

Paul Rudnick, author of The Most Fabulous Story Ever Told, *writes for stage and screen.*

On the set of 1961's *The Misfits* with husband Arthur Miller, who wrote the script; at right is co-star Clark Gable

Princess
Diana

Why could we not avert our eyes from her? Was it because she beckoned? Or was there something else we longed for?

By IAN BURUMA

WHAT WAS IT ABOUT DIANA, PRINCESS OF Wales, that brought such huge numbers of people from all walks of life literally to their knees after her death in 1997? What was her special appeal, not just to British subjects but also to people the world over? A late spasm of royalism hardly explains it, even in Britain, for many true British monarchists despised her for cheapening the royal institution by behaving more like a movie star or a pop diva than a princess. To many others, however, that was precisely her attraction.

Diana was beautiful, in a fresh-faced, English, outdoors-girl kind of way. She used her big blue eyes to their fullest advantage, melting your heart through an expression of complete vulnerability. Diana's eyes, like those of Marilyn Monroe, contained an appeal directed not to any individual but to the world at large. Please don't hurt me, they seemed to say. She often looked as if she were on the verge of tears, in the manner of folk images of the Virgin Mary. Yet she was one of the richest, most glamorous and socially powerful women in the world. This combination of vulnerability and power was perhaps her greatest asset.

Their fairy-tale wedding became tabloid fodder

Diana was a princess, but there are many princesses in Europe, none of whom ever came close to capturing the popular imagination the way she did. Princess Grace of Monaco was perhaps the nearest thing, but then she had really been a movie star, which surely provided the vital luster to her role as figurehead of a country that is little more than a gambling casino on the southern coast of France. The rather louche glamour of Monaco's royal family is nothing compared with the fading but still palpable grandeur of the British monarchy. To those who savor such things, British royals are the first among equals of world royalty, the last symbols of an aristocratic society that has largely disappeared but still hangs on, with much of its Victorian pomp intact, in Britain.

Diana not only married into the British monarchy but was the offspring of a family, the Spencers, that is at least as old as the British royal family and considers itself in some ways to be rather grander. It is not rare in England to hear the Spencers' Englishness compared favorably with the "foreign" (German) background of the Windsors. The famous, moving speech given by her younger brother, the Earl of Spencer, at

BORN July 1 in Sandringham, England

1961

A FAMILY haughtier than the Windsors: Diana Frances Spencer in 1968

1981 Marries Charles

1982 Prince William born

1984 Prince Harry born

1995 Diana discusses her marriage on TV

1992 Diana and Charles announce their separation

1993 Diana reveals her plan to withdraw from public life

1996 The divorce is finalized

1997

DIED Aug. 31, after a car crash in Paris

"I desperately loved my husband ... I thought we were a good team ... Here was a fairy story that everybody wanted to work."

DIANA on her failed marriage, from her BBC-TV interview

With her cherished sons William and Harry—the royal family's "heir and a spare"—in 1989

her funeral, with its barely contained hostility toward his royal in-laws, was an exercise of extraordinary hauteur.

So Diana had snob appeal to burn. But that alone would not have secured her popularity. Most of the people who worshipped her, who read every tidbit about her in the gossip press and hung up pictures of her in their rooms, were not social snobs. Like Princess Grace of Monaco, Diana was a celebrity royal. She was a movie star who never actually appeared in a movie; in a sense her whole life was a movie, a serial melodrama acted out in public, with every twist and turn of the plot reported to a world audience. Diana was astute enough to understand the power of television and the voracious British tabloid newspapers. And she consistently tried to use the mass media as a stage for projecting her image—as the wronged spouse, as the radiant society beauty, as the compassionate princess hugging AIDS patients and land-mine victims, and as the mourning princess crying at celebrity funerals.

However, like many celebrities before her, she found out that she couldn't turn the media on and off at will. The media needed her to feed the public appetite for celebrity gossip, and she needed them for her public performance, but what she hadn't bargained for was that her melodrama ran on without breaks. Everything she said or did was fair copy. After deliberately making her private life public, she soon discovered there was nothing private left.

In a sense, the quasi-religious mystique of royalty came full circle with Diana. Monarchy used to be based on divine right. But just as monarchy used religious trappings to justify its rule, modern show-biz celebrity has a way of slipping into a form of popular religion. It is surely not for nothing that an idolized pop singer of recent times so successfully exploited her given name, Madonna. One of the most traditional roles of religious idols is a sacrificial one; we project our sins onto them, and they bear our crosses in public.

Diana was a sacrificial symbol in several ways. First she became the patron saint of victims, the sick, the discriminated against, the homeless. Then, partly through her real suffering at the hands of a rigidly formal family trained to play rigidly formal public roles, and partly through her shrewd manipulation of the press, Diana projected a compelling image of victimhood. Women in unhappy marriages identified with her; so did outsiders of one kind or another, ethnic, sexual or social. Like many religious idols, she was openly abused and ridiculed, in her case by the same press that stoked the public worship of her. And finally she became the ultimate victim of her own fame: pursued by paparazzi, she became a twisted and battered body in a limousine. It was a fittingly tawdry end to what had become an increasingly tawdry melodrama. But it is in the nature of religion that forms change to fit the times. Diana—celebrity, tabloid princess, *mater dolorosa* of the pop and fashion scene—was, if nothing else, the perfect idol for our times. ∎

Ian Buruma is the author of The Wages of Guilt *and, most recently,* Anglomania.

Standing out in the hobnobbing mob at the Ascot races, 1989

Dancing with John Travolta at the Reagan White House, 1985

Visiting land-mine victim Sandra Tigica, 13, in Angola in 1997

Star Power: The Most Beautiful Women of the 20th Century

Theirs are the faces and figures that have launched millions of fantasies, spellbinding us with the power of pure pulchritude

The Elegant Pixie
Audrey Hepburn
It wasn't just that Audrey Hepburn had exquisite features and unimpeachable style. It was also her verve that made her so adorable

The Absolute Knockout
Liz Taylor
Liz Taylor's life hasn't been pretty, but her virtually violet eyes are. Her diamonds could barely compete

The Outré Sylph
Josephine Baker

Josephine Baker began as a comic but had beauty and the élan to be brazen about it. She was one of the century's first riot girls

The Dream Date
Cindy Crawford

Cindy Crawford has more of things: more hair, more cleavage, more lips and, let's face it, more cash. But especially more hair

The Classic Beauty
Grace Kelly

She earned her name, Grace. Her looks were perfection: creamy skin, lustrous hair. Her manner—a little untouchable—was, of course, fit for a prince

The Sex Kitten
Brigitte Bardot

The princess of pout, the countess of come hither, Brigitte Bardot exuded a carefree, naive sexuality that brought a whole new audience to French films

Star Power: The Most Attractive Men of the 20th Century

Take your pick—dreamboat, cowboy or libido-in-tuxedo—Hollywood found the faces that made hearts flare up when the lights went down

The Cool Rogue
Sean Connery
Connery, Sean Connery: the original and best James Bond is a man whose magnetism is undiminished by age

The Comic Charmer, '90s Edition
Will Smith
Will Smith, congenial charisma factory, inherits the mantle from Mr. Grant. Love those ears!

The Comic Charmer, '50s Edition
Cary Grant
Civilized, funny and built to wear a tux, Cary Grant had just the right amount of everything, including hair, lines and chin indentation

The Looker
Paul Newman
What god put the twinkle in those eyes? Paul Newman is a paradox: boyish and adult, sly and tender, he's the once and future dream date

The Dishy Imp
Tom Cruise
He has fine teeth, but it's really the wicked eyes and cheekbones that give this top gun his $20 million grin

The Sundance Kid
Robert Redford
It's hard for men to be both blond and rugged, but Robert Redford made it look easy. And romantic to boot. The Ur–Brad Pitt

American royalty: the clan in Britain, where Joseph Kennedy was U.S. ambassador to the Court of St. James's from 1937 to 1940

The
Kennedys

With its amalgam of political triumph and human tragedy, their saga enthralled the nation and made them America's most powerful family

By HUGH SIDEY

THE KENNEDY CLAN, THE PRE-EMINENT AMERICAN political family of our time, seems to be cast in the stars, the distant stuff of legend. But look down. They march ever more numerous among us. There's a spot on Washington's infamous Beltway where an unsuspecting family might find their children in school with a couple of Joseph and Rose Kennedy's 54 great-grandchildren. That same family could be the neighbors of Eunice Kennedy Shriver, one of the Kennedy clan's five surviving originals (there were nine). It could be served in the Maryland assembly by delegate Mark Shriver, nephew of the martyred John Kennedy (and one of 29 grandchildren of Joe and Rose). And it could fall under the

growing political hand of Kathleen Kennedy Townsend, oldest child of the murdered Robert Kennedy, now Maryland's lieutenant governor and touted for higher office.

Members of such a Beltway family would have as good a chance as not to pass Ethel Kennedy, Bobby's widow and still the exuberant duchess of Hickory Hill, while driving to work along the Potomac River parkways. And if in the media or a lobbying business (a reasonable likelihood in that neighborhood), he or she would sooner or later sit down with Massachusetts Senator Ted Kennedy or his son, Rhode Island Congressman Patrick Kennedy, now in the House Democratic leadership, to make a little political rain.

The Kennedy clan is embedded in American political

> **[It is the tale]** of a family that has managed to retain its bonds despite all the disintegrating forces of 20th century life.
>
> DORIS KEARNS GOODWIN, *The Kennedys and the Fitzgeralds*

No happy-ever-afterings: the nuptials of Jacqueline Bouvier

Before the fall: John and John Jr. lighten up the Oval Office

culture of the past half-century like no other family. They arrived at that power base through cold calculation and the blunt instrument of their immense wealth but also because of their honorable service to the nation, their reckless exuberance and glamour—and family tragedy beyond measure. The founding father of the clan, Joseph Kennedy, came from immigrant stock with all the eccentric genius and anger of his blighted kin, but he was touched by the magic of America. He went to the élitist Boston Latin School; on to Harvard; and then in the Roaring Twenties, with little regard for ethics or even the law, plunged into the worlds of banking and moviemaking. He cashed in before the market crash of 1929. When Franklin Roosevelt called Joe to Washington to clean up the Securities and Exchange Commission, somebody asked F.D.R. why he had tapped such a

crook. "Takes one to catch one," replied Roosevelt. Kennedy did a superb job.

When Joe's second son, John F. Kennedy, was ready to make his run for the presidency, the family fortune was estimated to be between $300 million and $500 million, one of the world's great private hoards. But by then, the moneymaking was clearly of secondary importance in the Kennedy ambitions. "None of my children give a damn about business," Joe said with pride. "The only thing that matters is family. I tell them that when they end this life, if they can count their friends on one hand, they will be lucky. Stick with family."

There was magic in that moment in history. Old Joe, whose methods and money were more suspect than ever, stayed out of sight while that handsome clan captivated

1888 Joseph P. Kennedy born in East Boston	1914 Joe Kennedy marries Rose Fitzgerald	1953 Jacqueline Bouvier weds J.F.K.		1968 R.F.K. assassinated; Jackie Kennedy marries Aristotle Onassis	1994 Jacqueline Kennedy Onassis dies
		1943 J.F.K.'s heroics save his crew at sea in Pacific war	1963 J.F.K. assassinated		
1888					
1891 Rose Fitzgerald born	1917 Second son John F. Kennedy born	1944 Eldest son Joe Jr. dies in crash in England	1961 J.F.K. inaugurated	1969 Ted Kennedy's Chappaquiddick crisis; Joe Kennedy dies	1995 Rose Kennedy dies
		1965 Robert and Edward Kennedy become first brothers to serve together in the Senate in 162 years			1999 John Kennedy Jr. and wife die in plane crash

At Robert's home, J.F.K. hurls a football at nephew Bobby Jr.

America. Rose and her daughters gave teas and speeches; Bobby ran Jack's campaign; and Ted gallivanted across the West riding broncos and making ski jumps. And the young Senator's wife Jackie shivered in the cold blasts of Wisconsin, wearing her designer sheaths and elbow-length shell gloves, beautiful, hushed and unyielding in her honesty about where she came from and who she was.

In power, the Kennedys strode over their failures—the Bay of Pigs, the Berlin Wall—with hardly a sidelong glance. John Kennedy's popularity grew, resting on eloquent speeches, his ravishing family and his toughness in national-security affairs and against racism as civil rights upheavals seized the nation. "Jack's the luckiest kid I know," rasped Old Joe one day after the dark summer of 1961. "He has learned most of the lessons of being President right at the start."

But the luck ran out in Dallas at noon on Nov. 22, 1963. Kennedy's assassination would cut short the promise, would unleash a Niagara of probes and books and movies, and suddenly Camelot would be tarnished with tawdry revelations about John Kennedy's careless sexual indulgences. But oddly, the legend of the Kennedy clan would soar above it all. There was enough honest devotion to the American ideal; there was enough honor and courage to carry it beyond the failures. The legend had been seared in the Dallas death throes. And then again in Los Angeles as a second brother fell. It was passed down as tribal wisdom to many children. It was the Holy Grail for the swelling ranks of the Kennedys themselves.

The family soldiered on, but all so human, no media blinders in this time. There was Chappaquiddick, the tragedy that disgraced Ted. And there was just plain dysfunction in the families of Old Joe's grandchildren, so often pictured as a healthy, endearing gene pool of American strength and enthusiasm—raucous but right. There were divorces, bizarre sexual escapades and weird accidents, all of them strewn across the tabloids and blared worldwide by the talk-show hosts. Nor were the tragedies over: in July 1999, John F. Kennedy Jr., the family's young Adonis, his elegant wife Carolyn Bessette Kennedy and her sister Lauren were killed in a plane crash at sea—with John at the controls.

But between the titillating interludes of scandal and the unexpected blows of tragedy is the fact that most of the 85 surviving members of the Kennedy clan live worthy lives. Most of the adults have advanced degrees of some sort. Virtually all the clan of proper age has been involved at some point in public service. The great fortune of Joe Kennedy has been divided into trusts, and while it provides the family with ease in education and travel, it does not put any of them in today's ranks of the superwealthy, the super-indolent, the superarrogant. The adventure of public service still is the clan's most powerful impulse. "More exciting than anything I've done," said Old Joe a long time ago. The call is heard unto the fourth generation. ■

Veteran White House correspondent Hugh Sidey has reported on and written about nine U.S. presidencies for TIME.

Charm and charisma: brothers Jack, Bobby and Ted in 1960

Tragic end: John Kennedy Jr. and wife Carolyn Bessette, 1997

Emmeline Pankhurst

The Victorian Englishwoman led the suffragist crusade, winning women the vote—and transforming society

By MARINA WARNER

NOT EVEN THE NOISIEST PROPONENTS OF WOMEN'S proper place back in the home could seriously suggest today that women should not have the vote. Yet "the mother half of the human family," in Emmeline Pankhurst's phrase, was fully enfranchised only in this century. In Britain, so proud to claim "the Mother of Parliaments," universal suffrage—including women's—was granted only in the year of her death, 1928. Mrs. Pankhurst was born a Victorian Englishwoman, but she shaped an idea of women for our time; she shook society into a new pattern from which there could be no going back.

The struggle to get votes for women, led by Mrs. Pankhurst and her daughter Christabel, who headed the militant suffragists, convulsed Britain from 1905 to 1914. The opposition the Liberal government put up looks incomprehensible today, and it provoked, among all classes and conditions of women, furious and passionate protests. The response of the police, the courts and sometimes the crowds of suffragist opponents still makes shocking reading. Women were battered in demonstrations and, during hunger strikes, brutally force-fed in prison. When these measures risked taking lives, the infamous Cat & Mouse Act was passed so that a weakened hunger striker would be released, then rearrested when strong enough to continue her sentence. Under it, Mrs. Pankhurst went to prison

12 times in 1912—when she was 54. No wonder she railed, "The militancy of men, through all the centuries, has drenched the world with blood. The militancy of women has harmed no human life save the lives of those who fought the battle of righteousness."

Mrs. Pankhurst's father was a Manchester manufacturer with radical sympathies. When she was small, she consumed *Uncle Tom's Cabin*, John Bunyan and abolitionist materials; her earliest memories included hearing Elizabeth Cady Stanton speak. Her father was keen on amateur theatricals in the home; his daughter later enthralled listeners with her oratory and her voice. The young Rebecca West described hearing Mrs. Pankhurst in full cry: "Trembling like a reed, she lifted up her hoarse, sweet voice on the platform, but the reed was of steel and it was tremendous."

Richard Pankhurst, whom she married in 1879, when she was 20 and he was 40, was a brilliant lawyer, selflessly dedicated to reform, who drafted pioneering legislation granting women independent control of their finances. Emmeline bore five children but lost two sons, and when Richard died suddenly in 1898, she was left to bring up her children alone, with no private means.

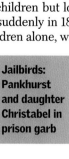

Jailbirds: Pankhurst and daughter Christabel in prison garb

The Pankhurst women formed an intrepid, determined, powerfully gifted band. In 1903 they founded the Women's Social and Political Union. It was, Emmeline Pankhurst wrote later, "simply a suffrage army in the field." The

BORN Emmeline Goulden, July 14, in Manchester, England

1903 Establishes the Women's Social and Political Union

1915 25,000 U.S. suffragists march in New York City

1920 Women win the vote in the U.S.

1928 Women's voting age lowered to 21 in Britain

1858

1928

1905 The W.S.P.U. adopts more militant tactics

1914 Shifts energy to supporting her country's effort in World War I

1918 Women over 30 vote for the first time in Britain

DIES June 14, 1928, in London

> ## We are driven to this. We are determined to go on with this agitation. It is our duty to make this world a better place.
>
> **EMMELINE PANKHURST, at the start of her campaign**

Not a leg to stand on: British police place the suffragist leader under arrest—again

The political leaders of Edwardian Britain were utterly confounded by the energy and violence of this female rebellion; by the barrage of mockery, interruptions and demands hurled; and, later, by the sight of viragoes in silk petticoats, matrons with hammers, ladies with stones in their kid gloves, mothers and mill girls unbowed before the forces of judges, policemen and prison wardens. Many suffragists in Britain and the U.S. argued that the Pankhursts' violence—arson, window smashing, picture slashing and hunger strikes—hurt the cause and fueled misogynistic views of female "hysteria." Though the question remains, the historical record shows shameless government procrastination, broken pledges and obstruction long before the suffragists abandoned heckling for acting up.

Mrs. Pankhurst took suffragist thinking far and wide: she even managed to slip in a lecture tour of the U.S. between spells of a Cat & Mouse jail sentence. To her, suffrage meant more than equality with men. While she was bent on sweeping away the limits of gender, she envisioned society transformed by feminine energies, above all by chastity, far surpassing the male's. In this, she is the foremother of the separatist wing of feminism today: the battle for the vote was for her a battle for the bedroom. She wrote, "We want to gain for [women] all the rights and protection that laws can give them. And, above all, we want the good influence of women to tell to its greatest extent in the social and moral questions of the time. But we cannot do this unless we have the vote and are recognised as citizens and voices to be listened to." She concluded her plea to a court in 1912 with the ringing declaration, "We are here, not because we are lawbreakers; we are here in our efforts to become lawmakers."

It is hard today not to sigh at the ardor of Emmeline Pankhurst's hope in what voting could achieve, not to be amazed at the confidence she showed in political reform. But heroism looks to the future, and heroes hold to their faith. Joan of Arc was the suffragists' mascot, Boadicea their goddess, and Mrs. Pankhurst the true inheritor of the armed maidens of heroic legend. ∎

charismatic, dictatorial eldest daughter Christabel emerged in her teens as the W.S.P.U.'s strategist and an indomitable activist, with nerves of tungsten. Mrs. Pankhurst's second daughter Sylvia, who was an artist, pioneered the corporate logo: as designer and scene painter of the W.S.P.U., she created banners, costumes and badges in the suffragist livery of white, purple and green. Though the family would eventually split over policy, their combined talents powered from the beginning an astonishingly versatile tactical machine.

THE W.S.P.U. ADOPTED A FRENCH-REVOLUTIONARY sense of crowd management, public spectacle and symbolic ceremony. They would greet one of their number on release from jail and draw her in triumph through the streets in a flower-decked wagon, and they staged elaborate allegorical pageants and torchlight processions. Their example was followed internationally: the U.S. suffragist Alice Paul, who had taken part in agitation while studying in London, brought militancy to the U.S., leading a march 5,000 strong in 1910.

Marina Warner's latest book is No Go the Bogeyman: Scaring, Lulling and Making Mock.

Rosa Parks

Her simple act of protest galvanized America's civil rights revolution

By RITA DOVE

> # "He spoke again and said, 'You'd better make it light on yourselves and let me have those seats.'"
>
> **ROSA PARKS**, in an interview, describing her arrest

How she sat there,
the time right inside a place
so wrong it was ready.

—From "Rosa," in *On the Bus with Rosa Parks* by Rita Dove

WE KNOW THE STORY. ONE DECEMBER EVENING, a woman left work and boarded a bus for home. She was tired; her feet ached. But this was Montgomery, Ala., in 1955, and as the bus became crowded, the woman, a black woman, was ordered to give up her seat to a white man. When she remained seated, that simple decision eventually led to the disintegration of institutionalized segregation in the South, ushering in a new era of the civil rights movement.

This, anyway, was the story I had heard from the time I was curious enough to eavesdrop on adult conversations. I was three years old when a white bus driver warned Rosa Parks, "Well, I'm going to have you arrested," and she replied, "You may go on and do so." As a child, I didn't understand how doing nothing had caused so much activity, but I recognized the template: David slaying the giant Goliath, or the boy who saved his village by sticking his finger in the dike. And perhaps it is precisely the lure of fairy-tale retribution that colors the lens we look back through. Parks was 42 years old when she refused to give up her seat. She has insisted that her feet were not aching; she was, by her own testimony, no more tired than usual. And she did not plan her fateful act: "I did not get on the bus to get arrested," she has said. "I got on the bus to go home."

Montgomery's segregation laws were complex: blacks were required to pay their fare to the driver, then get off and reboard through the back door. Sometimes the bus would drive off before the paid-up customers made it to the back entrance. If the white section was full and another white customer entered, blacks were required to give up their seats and move farther to the back; a black person was not even allowed to sit across the aisle from whites. These humiliations were compounded by the fact that two-thirds of the bus riders in Montgomery were black.

Parks was not the first to be detained for this offense. Eight months earlier, Claudette Colvin, 15, refused to give up her seat and was arrested. Black activists met with this

girl to determine if she would make a good test case—as secretary of the local N.A.A.C.P., Parks attended the meeting—but it was decided that a more "upstanding" candidate was necessary to withstand the scrutiny of the courts and the press. Then in October, a young woman named Mary Louise Smith was arrested; N.A.A.C.P. leaders rejected her too as their vehicle, looking for someone more able to withstand media scrutiny. Smith paid the fine and was released.

Six weeks later, the time was ripe. The facts, rubbed shiny for retelling, are these: On Dec. 1, 1955, Mrs. Rosa Parks, seamstress for the Montgomery Fair department store, boarded the Cleveland Avenue bus. She took a seat in the fifth row—the first row of the "Colored Section." The driver was the same one who had put her off a bus 12 years earlier for refusing to get off and reboard through the back door. ("He was still mean-looking," she has said.) Did that make her stubborn? Or had her work in the N.A.A.C.P. sharpened her sensibilities so that she knew what to do—or more precisely, what not to do: Don't frown, don't struggle, don't shout, don't pay the fine?

At the news of the arrest, local civil rights leader E.D. Nixon exclaimed, "My God, look what segregation has put

Parks in a Montgomery bus a year after her famous 1955 ride

BORN Rosa Louise McCauley, Feb. 4, in Tuskegee, Ala.

1913

1955 On Dec. 1 in Montgomery, Ala., she refuses to go to the back of the bus and is arrested, igniting bus boycott led by Martin Luther King Jr.

1956 Boycott ends on Dec. 21, after U.S. Supreme Court rules bus segregation is unconstitutional

1957 Moves to Michigan to escape harassment

1996 Receives Presidential Medal of Freedom

HONORED Receiving Congressional Gold Medal, 1999

in my hands!" Parks was not only above moral reproach (securely married, reasonably employed) but possessed a quiet fortitude as well as political savvy—in short, she was the ideal plaintiff for a test case.

Bail was posted by Clifford Durr, a white lawyer whose wife had employed Parks as a seamstress. That evening, after talking it over with her mother and husband, Parks agreed to challenge the constitutionality of Montgomery's segregation laws. During a midnight meeting of the Women's Political Council, 35,000 handbills were run off for distribution to all black schools the next morning.

The message was simple: "We are ... asking every Negro to stay off the buses Monday in protest of the

Despite her retiring public image, Parks was an activist who helped King lead the bus boycott

arrest and trial ... You can afford to stay out of school for one day. If you work, take a cab, or walk. But please, children and grown-ups, don't ride the bus at all on Monday."

Monday came. Rain threatened, yet the black population of Montgomery stayed off the buses, either walking or catching one of the black cabs stopping at every municipal bus stop for 10¢ per customer—standard bus fare. Meanwhile, Parks was scheduled to appear in court. As she made her way through the throngs at the courthouse, a demure figure in a long-sleeved black dress with white collar and cuffs, a trim black velvet hat, gray coat and white gloves, a girl in the crowd caught sight of her and cried out, "Oh, she's so sweet. They've messed with the wrong one now!"

Yes, indeed. The trial lasted 30 min., with the expected conviction and penalty. That afternoon, the Montgomery Improvement Association was formed. So as not to ruffle any local activists' feathers, the members elected as their president a relative newcomer to Montgomery, the young minister of Dexter Avenue Baptist Church: the Rev. Martin Luther King Jr. That evening, addressing a crowd gathered at the Holt Street Baptist Church, King declared in that sonorous, ringing voice millions the world over would soon thrill to: "There comes a time that people get tired." When he was finished, Parks stood up so the audience could see her. She did not speak; there was no need to. Here I am, her silence said, among you.

And she has been with us ever since—a persistent symbol of human dignity in the face of brutal authority. The famous U.P.I. photo (actually taken on Dec. 21, 1956, the

day Montgomery's public transit system was legally integrated) is a study of calm strength. She is looking out the bus window, her hands resting in the folds of her dress, while a white man sits, unperturbed, behind her. That clear profile, the neat cloche and eyeglasses and sensible coat—she could have been my mother, anybody's favorite aunt.

HISTORY IS OFTEN PORTRAYED AS A STRING OF ARIAS in a grand opera, all baritone intrigues and tenor heroics. Some of the most tumultuous events, however, have been provoked by serendipity—the assassination of an inconsequential archduke spawned World War I, a kicked-over lantern may have sparked the Great Chicago Fire. One cannot help wondering what role Martin Luther King Jr. would have played in the civil rights movement if the opportunity had not presented itself that first evening of the boycott—if Rosa Parks had chosen a row farther back from the outset, or if she had missed the bus altogether.

At the end of this millennium (and a particularly noisy century), it is the modesty of Rosa Parks' example that sustains us. It is no less than the belief in the power of the individual, that cornerstone of the American Dream, that she inspires, along with the hope that all of us—even the least of us—could be that brave, that serenely human, when crunch time comes. ∎

Rita Dove, former U.S. poet laureate, is the winner of the 1987 Pulitzer Prize for Poetry.

With Voices Raised

Among the eloquent advocates for black equality were rebels, preachers, dreamers, and an opera singer

Jesse Jackson

The passionate minister was the first black to stage a persuasive run for the presidency, in 1984. "White folks don't want peace; they want quiet. The price you pay for peace is justice. Until there is justice, there will be no peace and quiet."

Marian Anderson

Her 1939 performance at the Lincoln Memorial galvanized the nation. "As long as you keep a person down, some part of you has to be down there to hold him down, so it means you cannot soar as you otherwise might."

Malcolm X

The Black Muslim leader posed a challenge to the integrationist ideals of other civil rights groups. "I believe in the brotherhood of all men, but I don't believe in wasting brotherhood on anyone who doesn't want to practice it with me. Brotherhood is a two-way street."

W.E.B. Du Bois

A true pioneer, he was a co-founder of the National Association for the Advancement of Colored People. "Cannot the nation that has absorbed 10 million foreigners absorb 10 million Negroes?"

Harvey Milk

People told him no openly gay man could win political office in America—even in San Francisco. Fortunately, he ignored them

By JOHN CLOUD

Che Guevara

Though his brand of communism has lost its fire, he remains a potent symbol of rebellion and an alluring avatar of revolution

By ARIEL DORFMAN

BY THE TIME ERNESTO GUEVARA, KNOWN TO US AS Che, was murdered in the jungles of Bolivia in October 1967, he was already a legend to my generation, not only in Latin America but also around the world. And like so many epics, the story of the obscure Argentine doctor who abandoned his profession and his native land to pursue the emancipation of the poor of the earth began with a voyage.

In 1956, along with Fidel Castro and a handful of others, Che had crossed the Caribbean in the rickety yacht *Granma* on the mad mission of invading Cuba and overthrowing the dictator Fulgencio Batista. Landing in a hostile swamp, losing most of their contingent, the survivors fought their way to the Sierra Maestra. A bit over two years later, after a guerrilla campaign in which Guevara displayed such outrageous bravery and skill that he was named comandante, the insurgents entered Havana and launched what was to become the first and only victorious socialist revolution in the Americas. The images were thereafter invariably gigantic. Che the titan standing up to the *Yanquis*, the world's dominant power. Che the moral guru proclaiming that a New

Castro and Che in 1960. While Fidel reshaped Cuba, Che left to spread the revolution abroad

Man, no ego and all ferocious love for the other, had to be forcibly created out of the ruins of the old one. Che the romantic mysteriously leaving the revolution to continue, sick though he might be with asthma, the struggle against oppression and tyranny.

His execution in Vallegrande at the age of 39 only enhanced Guevara's mythical stature. That Christ-like figure laid out on a bed of death with his uncanny eyes almost about to open; those fearless last words ("Shoot, coward, you're only going to kill a man") that somebody invented or reported; the anonymous burial and the hacked-off hands, as if his killers feared him more after he was dead than when he had been alive: all of it is scalded into the mind and memory of those defiant times. He would resurrect, young people shouted in the late '60s; I can remember fervently proclaiming it in the streets of Santiago, Chile, while similar vows exploded across Latin America. *¡No lo vamos a olvidar!* We won't let him be forgotten.

More than 30 years later, the dead hero has indeed persisted in collective memory, but not in the way most of us would have anticipated. Che has become ubiquitous: he

BORN Ernesto Guevara de la Serna, June 14, in Rosario, Argentina

1966 Attempts guerrilla revolution in Bolivia

1965 Leaves Cuba to lead insurrections abroad

1958 Leads guerrillas in decisive battle

1928

1967

1956 Joins Castro in Mexico and sails with his forces to Cuba

1959 Becomes part of new Cuban regime

EXECUTED Oct. 9, after his capture by the Bolivian army

CHE is "Adolfo Mena" in this fake Uruguayan passport

> ## Always be capable of feeling ... any injustice committed against anyone anywhere in the world.
>
> CHE GUEVARA, in his goodbye letter to his children

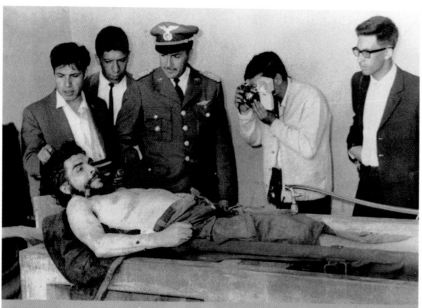

Che's execution in Bolivia in 1967 sealed his legend as a martyr of the revolution

stares out at us from coffee mugs and posters, jingles at the end of key rings and jewelry, pops up in rock songs and operas and art shows. This apotheosis of his image has been accompanied by a parallel disappearance of the real man, swallowed by the myth. Most of those who idolize the incendiary guerrilla with the star on his beret were born long after his demise and have only the sketchiest knowledge of his goals or his life. Gone is the generous Che who tended wounded enemy soldiers, gone is the vulnerable warrior who wanted to curtail his love of life lest it make him less effective in combat, and gone also is the darker, more turbulent Che who signed orders to execute prisoners in Cuban jails without a fair trial.

THIS ERASURE OF COMPLEXITY IS THE NORMAL FATE of any icon. More paradoxical is that the humanity that worships Che has by and large turned away from just about everything he believed in. The future he predicted has not been kind to his ideals or his ideas. Back in the '60s, we presumed that his self-immolation would be commemorated by social action, the downtrodden rising against the system and creating—to use Che's own words—two, three, many Vietnams. Thousands of luminous young men, particularly in Latin America, followed his example into the hills and were slaughtered there or tortured to death in sad city cellars, never knowing that their dreams of total liberation, like those of Che, would not come true. If Vietnam is being imitated today, it is primarily as a model for how a society forged in insurrection now seeks to be integrated into the global market. Nor has Guevara's uncompromising, unrealistic style of struggle, or his ethical absolutism, prevailed. The major revolutions of the past quarter-century (South Africa, Iran, the Philippines,

Nicaragua), not to mention the peaceful transitions to democracy in Latin America, East Asia and the communist world, have all entailed negotiations with former adversaries, a give-and-take that could not be farther from Che's unyielding demand for confrontation to the death. Even Subcomandante Marcos, the spokesman for the Chiapas Maya revolt, whose charisma and moral stance remind us of Che's, does not espouse his hero's economic or military theories.

How to understand, then, Che Guevara's pervasive popularity, especially among the affluent young?

Perhaps in these orphaned times of incessantly shifting identities and alliances, the fantasy of an adventurer who altered countries and crossed borders and broke down limits without betraying his basic loyalties offers the restless youth of our era an optimal combination, grounding them in a fierce center of moral gravity while simultaneously appealing to their nomadic impulse. To those who will never follow in his footsteps, submerged as they are in a world of cynicism, self-interest and frantic consumption, nothing could be more vicariously gratifying than Che's disdain for material comfort and everyday desires. Perhaps it is Che's distance, the impossibility of duplicating his life anymore, that makes him so attractive. Is it conceivable that one of the only two Latin Americans named to the TIME 100 is a comfortable symbol of rebellion precisely because he is no longer dangerous?

I wouldn't be too sure. I suspect that the young of the world grasp that the man whose poster beckons from their walls cannot be that irrelevant, this secular saint ready to die because he could not tolerate a world where *los pobres de la tierra*, the displaced and dislocated of history, would be eternally relegated to its vast margins.

Even though I have come to be wary of dead heroes and the overwhelming burden their martyrdom imposes on the living, I will allow myself a prophecy. Or maybe it is a warning. More than 3 billion human beings on this planet right now live on less than $2 a day. And every day that breaks, 40,000 children—more than one every second!—succumb to diseases linked to chronic hunger. They are there, always there, the terrifying conditions of injustice and inequality that led Che many decades ago to start his journey toward that bullet and that photo awaiting him in Bolivia.

The powerful of the earth should take heed: deep inside that T shirt where we have tried to trap him, the eyes of Che Guevara are still burning with impatience. ∎

Ariel Dorfman holds the Walter Hines Page Chair at Duke University. His latest novel is The Nanny and the Iceberg.

Andrei
Sakharov

Speaking truth to power, he became the conscience of the cold
war and inspired the movement that toppled Soviet communism

By FANG LIZHI WITH ROMESH RATNESAR

His Moscow home was a refuge for democracy advocates

IN THE FALL OF 1962, WHEN HIS LIFE TOOK ITS FATEFUL turn, Andrei Sakharov was not yet known to the world. He was 41 years old, a decorated Soviet physicist developing nuclear weapons of terrifying power deep in the heart of the Soviet Union. The U.S. and the U.S.S.R. were locked in a frenzied contest for nuclear superiority. That September the Kremlin was to conduct two massive atmospheric tests of bombs that Sakharov had helped design. Sakharov feared the radioactive fallout from the second test would kill hundreds of thousands of civilians. He had also come to believe that another nuclear demonstration would only accelerate the arms race. He became desperate not to see his research used for reckless ends. On Sept. 25, he phoned Soviet Prime Minister Nikita Khrushchev. "The test is pointless," he said. "It will kill people for no reason." Khrushchev assured Sakharov he would inquire about postponing the

test. The very next day the detonation went off as planned.

Sakharov wept. "After that," he said, "I felt myself another man. I broke with my surroundings. I understood there was no point arguing." Thus began a journey that would make Sakharov the world's most famous political dissident and ultimately the inspiration for the democratic movement that doomed the Soviet Empire. Sakharov realized that the ideals he had pursued as a scientist—compassion, freedom, truth—could not coexist with the specter of the arms race or thrive under the authoritarian grip of state communism. "That was probably the most terrible lesson of my life," he wrote. "You can't sit on two chairs at once."

So Sakharov abandoned his cocooned life as his country's leading physicist to risk everything in battle against the two great threats to civilization in the second half of this

BORN May 21
in Moscow

1948 Begins work
on H-bomb project

1957 Writes papers on the
dangers of nuclear testing

1975 Wins
Nobel Prize

1986 Exile
ended by
Gorbachev

1921

1989

1953 First Soviet
H-bomb detonated

1968 Barred from all
military research

1980 Banished to Gorky
for denouncing Soviet
invasion of Afghanistan

DIES Dec. 14
in Moscow

" We should not minimize our sacred endeavors in this world, where, like faint glimmers in the dark, we have emerged ... **"**

SAKHAROV, in the Nobel speech delivered by his wife

century: nuclear war and communist dictatorship. In the dark, bitter depths of the cold war, Sakharov's voice rang out. "A miracle occurred," Aleksandr Solzhenitsyn wrote, "when Andrei Sakharov emerged in the Soviet state, among the swarms of corrupt, venal, unprincipled intelligentsia." By the time of his death in 1989, this humble physicist had influenced the spread of democratic ideals throughout the communist world. His moral challenge to tyranny, his faith in the individual and the power of reason, his courage in the face of denunciation and, finally, house arrest—made him a hero to ordinary citizens everywhere. He embodied the role that intellectuals are called upon to play in the creation of civil society and inspired scientists working under other dictatorships, including myself in China, to become leaders in the struggle for democracy.

In an age of constant technological change, Sakharov reminded the world that science is inseparable from conscience. He believed that science was a force for rationality and, from there, democracy: that in politics, as in science, objective truths can be arrived at only through a testing of hypotheses, a democratic consensus "based on a profound study of facts, theories and views, presupposing unprejudiced and open discussion." As a physicist, he believed that physical laws are immutable, applying to all things in nature. As a result, he regarded certain human values—such as liberty and the respect for individual dignity—as inviolable and universal. It is not surprising that in China today, many of the most outspoken advocates of political reform are members of the scientific and academic communities. They are all the progeny of Andrei Sakharov.

He was a most unlikely activist. Born in Moscow in 1921, Sakharov was groomed less for political protest than for scholarly solitude. He taught himself to read at four, and his father often demonstrated physics experiments ("miracles I could understand") to him as a child. At Moscow University in the 1940s, Sakharov was tabbed as one of the U.S.S.R.'s brightest young minds. After earning his doctorate, he was sent to a top-secret installation to spearhead the development of the hydrogen bomb. By 1953 the Soviets had detonated one. It was "the most terrible weapon in human history," Sakharov later wrote. Yet he felt that by building the H-bomb, "I was working for peace, that my work would help foster a balance of power."

His growing awareness of the deadly effects of nuclear fallout soon turned him against proliferation. His efforts to persuade Khrushchev to halt tests in the late '50s and early '60s resulted in the 1963 U.S.-Soviet treaty banning nuclear explosions in space, in the atmosphere and underwater. Khrushchev later called Sakharov "a crystal of morality"—but still one that could not be tolerated within the regime. The Kremlin took away his security privileges and ended his career as a nuclear physicist. But, Sakharov later said, "the atomic issue was a natural path into political issues." He campaigned for disarmament and turned his attention to the Soviet system, denouncing its stagnancy and intolerance of dissent. So uncompromising was his critique of the regime that it estranged him from his children.

OUTSIDE THE SOVIET UNION, EVEN IN CHINA, where his writings were predictably banned by the government, Sakharov's name and struggle were familiar to intellectuals and dissidents forging their own fights against authority. He received the Nobel Peace Prize in 1975, and in 1980 his arrest and exile to the remote city of Gorky (now called Nizhni Novgorod) made him a martyr. His refusal to be silenced even in banishment added to his legend. Then came the rousing finale: his release and hero's return to Moscow in 1986; his relentless prodding of Mikhail Gorbachev to pursue democratization; and his election to the Congress of People's Deputies, the U.S.S.R.'s first democratically chosen body. At the time of his death, a tidal wave of democracy that the physicist had helped create was about to engulf the communist world.

What is Sakharov's legacy? With the cold war ended and the Soviet threat gone, his exhortations against totalitarianism might seem anachronistic. Yet in China, where political freedom continues to be suppressed and intellectuals face harassment and arrest, his voice is still one of encouragement. For scientists his career remains a model

Thousands of Russians paid tribute at Sakharov's funeral

of the moral responsibility that must accompany innovation. And Sakharov might remind the West too that freedom is fragile, that if democratic societies do not protect their liberties, even they may lose them. On the night of his death, after a tempestuous meeting of the Congress of People's Deputies, Sakharov told his wife Yelena Bonner, "Tomorrow there will be a battle!" That battle—at its core, the battle of individuals striving to shape their own destinies—must continue to be fought in the century to come. ∎

Chinese astrophysicist Fang Lizhi helped inspire the Tiananmen Square demonstrations in Beijing in 1989.

Billy Graham

Transcending doctrine and denomination, he has served as America's spiritual counselor and has made the U.S. safe for public testimonies of faith

By HAROLD BLOOM

WILLIAM FRANKLIN GRAHAM JR., KNOWN TO all the world as Billy, was 80 years old in 1999, and had been our leading religious revivalist for almost exactly 50 years, ever since his eight-week triumph in Los Angeles in the autumn of 1949. Indeed, for at least 40 years, Graham has been the Pope of Protestant America (if Protestant is still the right word). Graham's finest moment may have been when he appeared at President Bush's side, Bible in hand, as we commenced our war against Iraq in 1991. The great revivalist's presence symbolized that the gulf crusade was, if not Christian, at least biblical. Bush was not unique among our Presidents in displaying Graham. Eisenhower and Kennedy began the tradition of consulting the evangelist, but Johnson, Nixon and Ford intensified the practice that concluded with Bush's naming him "America's pastor." President Clinton has increasingly preferred the Rev. Jesse Jackson, but the aura of apostle still hovers around Billy Graham. Harry Truman unkindly proclaimed Graham a "counterfeit," a mere publicity monger, but while I still remain a Truman Democrat, I think our last really good President oversimplified the Graham phenomenon.

No one has accused Graham of intellectualism, profound spirituality or social compassion, but he is free of any association with the Christian right of Pat Robertson, Ralph Reed and all the other advocates of a God whose prime concerns are abolishing the graduated income tax and a woman's right to choose abortion (which Graham also opposes). And there have been no scandals, financial or sexual, to darken Graham's mission. His sincerity, transparent and convincing, cannot be denied. He is an icon essential to a country in which, for two centuries now, religion has been not the opiate but the poetry of the people. In the U.S., 96% of us believe in God, 90% pray, and 90% believe God loves them, according to Gallup polls. Graham is totally representative of American religious universalism. You don't run for office among us by proclaiming your skepticism or by deprecating Billy Graham.

Still, one can ask how so theatrical a preacher became central to the U.S. of the past half-century. Always an authentic revivalist, Graham has evaded both doctrine and denomination. He sounds not at all like a Fundamentalist, though he affirms the fundamentals— the literal truth of the Bible: the virgin birth, atoning death and the bodily resurrection of Christ; the Second Coming; salvation purely through grace by faith and not works. Graham's most important book, *Peace with God* (1953), is light-years away from C.S. Lewis' *Mere Christianity*, so revered by Fundamentalists. Everything that is harsh in Lewis is softened by Graham, whose essential optimism is inconsistent with his apocalyptic expectations. But you cannot read *Peace with God* and expect consistency; soft-edged Fundamentalism, Graham's stance, will not sustain scrutiny.

"God's machine gun" electrifies a capacity crowd of 16,000 at Pelican Stadium in New Orleans, 1954

Graham's coherence and significance depend upon the history of modern evangelical revivalism in the U.S. That history began with Charles Grandison Finney, who created a new American form of religious revival, a highly organized, popular spectacle. (He later gave up his career as an evangelist to become president of Oberlin College in 1851.) The tradition was carried on by Dwight Lyman Moody, William Ashley Sunday and Graham, the disciple of Moody rather than of Billy Sunday. Moody, in Finney's wake,

BORN Nov. 7, near Charlotte, N.C.

1949 William Randolph Hearst orders positive stories on Graham's L.A. crusade in his papers

1954 First overseas crusade, in Britain

1957 First televised crusade

1969 Offers prayer at Nixon Inauguration

1996 Receives Congressional Gold Medal

1918

1934 Attends revival meeting, decides to commit life to Christ

1950 Establishes the Billy Graham Evangelistic Association; launches *The Hour of Decision* radio show

1957 More than 2 million people attend 16-week crusade in New York City

> # When you went into the ministry, politics lost one of its potentially greatest practitioners.

RICHARD NIXON to Graham

invented methods and organizing principles that Graham would perfect: advancemen, advertising, aggressive publicity campaigns, and a staff of specialists (prayer leaders, singers, counselors, ushers). Graham perfected Moody's transformation of revivalism into mass popular entertainment, superbly executed in the New York City crusade of 1957, with triumphant performances at Yankee Stadium and Madison Square Garden.

Politics could have been the destructive element for Graham, since he started his rise in the age of Eisenhower and for a time was a fervent red hunter, an admirer of Senator Joe McCarthy's and an overall basher of the left, as here in a radio broadcast of 1953: "While nobody likes a watchdog, and for that reason many investigation committees are unpopular, I thank God for men who, in the face of public denouncement and ridicule, go loyally on in their work of exposing the pinks, the lavenders and the reds who have sought refuge beneath the wings of the American eagle and from that vantage point try in every subtle, undercover way to bring comfort, aid and help to the greatest enemy we have ever known—communism."

That is now a period piece, but I think it is important to keep it on the record. Graham, a slow but sure learner, moved with the spirit of the age, and in the 1980s he became a preacher of world peace, urging reconciliation

with Russia and China, where his wife Ruth, the daughter of missionaries, was born. Angry Fundamentalists turned against him, a move that became an anti-Graham passion when he rejected the program of the Christian right: "I don't think Jesus or the Apostles took sides in the political arenas of their day." The break between Graham and the Christian right became absolute when he denounced the violence of the antiabortion group Operation Rescue. "The tactics," Graham declared, "ought to be prayer and discussion."

THOUGH GRAHAM HAS NEVER, TO MY KNOWLEDGE, spoken out on behalf of the poor, it seems legitimate to conclude that his almost exclusive emphasis upon soul saving is his passionate center, even his authentic obsession. And there, whatever his inadequacies of intellect or of spiritual discernment, Graham has ministered to a particular American need: the public testimony of faith. He is the recognized leader of what continues to call itself American evangelical Protestantism, and his life and activities have sustained the self-respect of that vast entity. If there is an indigenous American religion—and I think there is, quite distinct from European Protestantism—then Graham remains its prime emblem.

Evangelicals constitute about 40% of Americans, and the same number believe God speaks to them directly. Such a

belief yearns for a purer and more primitive church than anyone is likely to see, and something in Graham retains the nostalgia for that purity. In old age and in poor health, he is anything but a triumphalist. There is no replacement for him, though he has hopes for his son Franklin. More than a third of our nation continues to believe in salvation only through a regeneration founded upon personal conversion to the Gospel, and Graham epitomizes that belief. A great showman, something of a charismatic, Graham exploited his gifts as an offering to America's particular way with the spirit. Some might have wished for more, but Graham honestly recognized his limitations, and his career nears its close with poignancy and a sense of achievement. ■

Harold Bloom is the author of The American Religion *and* Shakespeare: The Invention of the Human.

Graham, who suffers from Parkinson's disease, with his wife Ruth in 1993

Bill

W.

Out of the rubble of a wasted life, he overcame alcoholism and then founded a program that has helped millions of others do the same

By SUSAN CHEEVER

SECOND LIEUT. BILL WILSON DIDN'T THINK TWICE when the first butler he had ever seen offered him a drink. The 22-year-old soldier didn't think about how alcohol had destroyed his family. He didn't think about the Yankee temperance movement of his childhood or his loving fiancé Lois Burnham or his emerging talent for leadership. He didn't think about anything at all. "I had found the elixir of life," he wrote. Wilson's last drink, 17 years later, when alcohol had destroyed his health and his career, precipitated an epiphany that would change his life and the lives of millions of other alcoholics. Incarcerated for the fourth time at Manhattan's Towns Hospital in 1934, Wilson had a spiritual awakening—a flash of white light, a liberating awareness of God—that led to the founding of Alcoholics Anonymous and Wilson's revolutionary 12-step program, the successful remedy for alcoholism. The 12 steps have also generated successful programs for eating disorders, gambling, narcotics dependency, debting, sex addiction and people affected by others' addictions. Aldous Huxley called him "the greatest social architect of our century."

William Griffith Wilson grew up in a quarry town in Vermont. When he was 10, his hard-drinking father headed for Canada, and his mother moved to Boston, leaving the sickly child with her parents. As a soldier, and then as a businessman, Wilson drank to alleviate his depressions and to celebrate his Wall Street success. Married in 1918, he and Lois toured the country on a motorcycle and appeared to be a

promising young couple. By 1933, however, they were living on charity in her parents' house on Clinton Street in Brooklyn, N.Y. Wilson had become an unemployable drunk who disdained religion and even panhandled for cash.

Inspired by a friend who had stopped drinking, Wilson went to meetings of the Oxford Group, an evangelical society founded in Britain by an American. And as Wilson underwent a barbiturate-and-belladonna cure called "purge and puke"—state-of-the-art alcoholism treatment at the time—his brain spun with phrases from Oxford Group meetings, Carl Jung and William James' *Varieties of Religious Experience*, which he read in the hospital. Five sober months later, Wilson went to Akron, Ohio, on business. The deal fell through, and he wanted a drink. He stood in the lobby of the Mayflower Hotel, entranced by the sounds of the bar across the hall. Suddenly he became convinced that by helping another alcoholic, he could save himself.

Through a series of desperate telephone calls, he found Dr. Robert Smith, a skeptical drunk whose family persuaded him to give Wilson 15 minutes. Their meeting lasted for hours. A month later, Dr. Bob had his last drink, and that date, June 10, 1935, is the official birth date of A.A., which is based on the idea that only an alcoholic can help another alcoholic. "Because of our kinship in suffering," Bill wrote, "our channels of contact have always been charged with the language of the heart."

The Burnham house on Clinton Street became a haven for drunks. "My name is Bill W., and I'm an alcoholic," he

	1918 Marries Lois		1938 Forms the	1939 Publishes	1953 Publishes *Twelve*
BORN Nov.	Burnham. In 1951 she		Alcoholics Foundation	the book *Alcoholics*	*Steps and Twelve*
26 in East	founds Al-Anon for			*Anonymous,* which	*Traditions,* outlining a
Dorset, Vt.	families of alcoholics	1934 Takes his last drink		includes the 12 steps	structure for A.A.

1895 ── **1971**

1933 First of four hospitalizations for alcoholism

1935 Persuades Dr. Robert Smith to stay sober with him. This is the first A.A. meeting

WILSON in 1948, during a visit to A.A. groups in Canada

DIES Jan. 24, of pneumonia, in Miami

> ## " In the wake of my spiritual experience there came a vision of a society of alcoholics. "
>
> **BILL WILSON, writing to Carl Jung in 1961**

told assorted houseguests and visitors at meetings. To spread the word, he began writing down his principles for sobriety. Each chapter was read by the Clinton Street group and sent to Smith in Akron for more editing. The book had a dozen provisional titles, among them *The Way Out* and *The Empty Glass.* Edited to 400 pages, it was finally called *Alcoholics Anonymous*, and this became the group's name.

BUT THE BOOK, ALTHOUGH WELL REVIEWED, WASN'T selling. Wilson tried unsuccessfully to make a living as a wire-rope salesman. A.A. had about a hundred members, but many were still drinking. Meanwhile, in 1939, the bank foreclosed on the Clinton Street house, and the couple began years of homelessness, living as guests in borrowed rooms and at one point staying in temporary quarters above the A.A. clubhouse on 24th Street in Manhattan. In 1940 John D. Rockefeller Jr. held an A.A. dinner and was impressed enough to create a trust to provide Wilson with $30 a week—but no more. The tycoon felt that money would corrupt the group's spirit.

Then, in March 1941, the *Saturday Evening Post* published an article on A.A., and suddenly thousands of letters and requests poured in. Attendance at meetings doubled and tripled. Wilson had reached his audience. In *Twelve Traditions*, Wilson set down the suggested bylaws of Alcoholics Anonymous. In them, he created an enduring blueprint for an organization with a maximum of individual freedom and no accumulation of power or money. Public anonymity ensured humility. No contributions were required; no member could contribute more than $1,000.

Today more than 2 million A.A. members in 150 countries hold meetings in church basements, hospital conference rooms and school gyms, following Wilson's informal structure. Members identify themselves as alcoholics and share their stories; there are no rules or entry requirements, and many members use only first names.

Wilson believed the key to sobriety was a change of heart. The suggested 12 steps include an admission of powerlessness, a moral inventory, a restitution for harm done, a call to service and a surrender to some personal God—who can be anything from a radiator to a patriarch. Influenced by A.A., the American Medical Association has redefined alcoholism as a chronic disease, not a failure of willpower.

As Alcoholics Anonymous grew, Wilson became its principal symbol. He helped create a governing structure for the program and turned over his power. "I have become a pupil of the A.A. movement rather than the teacher," he wrote. A smoker into his 70s, he died of pneumonia and emphysema in Miami, where he went for treatment in 1971. To the end, he clung to the principles and the power of anonymity. He was always Bill W., refusing to take money for counseling and leadership. He turned down many honors, including a degree from Yale. And he declined TIME's offer to put him on the cover—even with his back turned. ■

Susan Cheever, a novelist and memoirist, is the author of Note Found in a Bottle: My Life as a Drinker.

At the 1955 A.A. convention in St. Louis, Mo., Wilson turned the leadership of the group over to its members

Person of the Century

The century's dominant themes—the ascent of science, the quest for human rights and the struggle to preserve democracy— were embodied by three larger-than-life figures

Who
Mattered
& Why

By **WALTER ISAACSON**

What an amazing cast of characters! What a wealth of heroes and villains to choose from! Some shook the world by arriving: Gandhi at the sea to make salt, Lenin at the Finland Station. Others by refusing to depart: Rosa Parks from her seat on the bus, that kid from the path of the tank near Tiananmen Square.

There were magical folks who could make freedom radiate through the walls of a Birmingham jail, a South African prison or a Gdansk shipyard.

Others made machines that could fly and machines that could think, discovered a mold that conquered infections and a molecule that formed the basis of life. There were people who could inspire us with a phrase: fear itself, tears and sweat, ask not. Frighten us with a word: *heil!* Or revise the universe with an equation: $E=mc^2$.

So how can we go about choosing the Person of the Century, the one who, for better or worse, personified our times and will be recorded by history as having the most lasting significance?

Let's begin by noting what our century will be remembered for. Out of the fog of proximity, three great themes emerge:

- The grand struggle between totalitarianism and democracy.
- The ability of courageous individuals to resist authority in order to secure their civil rights.
- The explosion of scientific and technical knowledge that unveiled the mysteries of the universe and helped ensure the triumph of freedom by unleashing the power of free minds and free markets.

The Century of Democracy

SOME PEOPLE, LOOKING AT THE FIRST OF THESE themes, sorrowfully insist that the choice has to be Hitler, Führer of the fascist genocides and refugee floods that plagued the century. He wrought the Holocaust that redefined evil and the war that reordered the world. Competing with him for such devilish distinction is Lenin, who snatched from obscurity the 19th century ideology of communism and devised the modern tools of totalitarian brutality. He begat not only Stalin and Mao but in some ways also Hitler, who was enchanted by the Soviets' terror tactics.

Doesn't the presence of such evil—and the continued eruption of totalitarian brutality from Uganda to Kosovo—mock the rationalists' faith that progress makes civilizations more civilized? Isn't Hitler, alas, the person who most influenced and symbolized this most genocidal of centuries?

No. He lost. So did Lenin and Stalin. Along with the others in their evil pantheon, and the totalitarian ideologies they represented, they are destined for the ash heap of history. If you had to describe the century's geopolitics in one sentence, it could be a short one: Freedom won. Free minds and free markets prevailed over fascism and communism.

So a more suitable choice would be someone who embodied the struggle for freedom: Franklin Roosevelt, the only person to be TIME's Man of the

Year thrice (for 1932, 1934 and 1941). He helped save capitalism from its most serious challenge, the Great Depression. And then he rallied the power of free people and free enterprise to defeat fascism.

Other great leaders were part of this process. Winston Churchill stood up to Hitler even earlier than Roosevelt did, when it took far more courage. Harry Truman, a plain-spoken man with gut instincts for what was right, forcefully began the struggle against Soviet expansionism, a challenge that Roosevelt was too sanguine about. Ronald Reagan and Mikhail Gorbachev helped choreograph the conclusion of that sorry empire's strut upon the stage. So too did Pope John Paul II, a Pole with a passion for both faith and freedom. And if you were to pick a hero who embodied America's contribution to winning the fight for freedom, it would probably be not Roosevelt, but instead the American G.I.

Nor is it proper to mythologize Roosevelt. The New Deal was at times a hodgepodge of conflicting economic ideas, marked more by enthusiasm than by coherence. It restored Americans' faith and hopes, saved them from fear itself, but never managed to end the Depression. The war did that.

Nevertheless, Franklin Roosevelt stands out among the century's political leaders. With his first-class temperament, wily manipulations and passion for experimentation, he's the jaunty face of democratic values. Thus we pick him as the era's foremost statesman and one of three finalists for Person of the Century. That may seem, to non-Americans, parochial. True, but this was, as our magazine's founder Henry Luce dubbed it in 1941, the American Century—politically, militarily, economically and ideologically.

When Roosevelt took office at the beginning of 1933 (the same week that Hitler assumed emergency powers in Germany), unemployment in the U.S. had, in three years, jumped from 4 million to 12 million, at least a quarter of the work force. Fathers of hungry kids were trying to sell apples on the street. Many of F.D.R.'s bold experiments ("Above all, try something") failed, but he brought hope to millions and some lasting contributions to the nation's foundation: Social Security, minimum wages, the right to join unions, insured bank deposits. Henceforth the national government (in the U.S. and most everywhere else) took on the duty of managing the economy and providing a social safety net.

By New Year's Day of 1941, the Depression still lingered, and the threat from Hitler was growing. Roosevelt went to his second-floor White House study to draft the address that would launch his unprecedented third term. There was a long silence, uncomfortably long, as his speechwriters waited. Then he leaned forward and began dictating. "We look forward to a world founded upon four essential human freedoms," he said. He proceeded to list them:

freedom of expression, freedom of worship, freedom from want, freedom from fear. One of the great themes of this century was the progress mankind has made toward each of them.

ROOSEVELT MADE ANOTHER enduring contribution: he escorted onto the century's stage a remarkable woman, his wife Eleanor. She was his counterpoint: uncompromisingly moral, earnest rather than devious, she became an icon of feminism and social justice in a nation just discovering the need to grant rights to women, blacks, ordinary workers and the poor. She discovered the depth of racial discrimination while touring New Deal programs (on a visit to Birmingham in 1938, she refused to sit in the white section of the auditorium), and subsequently peppered her husband with questions over dinner and memos at bedtime. Even after her husband's death, she remained one of the century's most powerful advocates for social fairness.

One political leader who rivals Roosevelt in embodying freedom's fight is Winston Churchill, who turned the world's darkest moments into Britain's finest hour. He despised tyranny with such a passion that he, and by extension his nation, was willing to stand alone against Hitler when it was most critical. And unlike Roosevelt, he came early to the crusade against Soviet tyranny as well. His eloquent speeches buttressed the faith of all freedom-loving people in both the righteousness of their struggle and the inevitability of their cause.

So why is he not Person of the Century? He was, after all, TIME's Man of the Half-Century in 1950. Well, the passage of time can alter our perspective. A lot has happened since 1950. It has become clear that one of the great themes of the century has been the success of those who resisted authority in order to seek civil rights, decolonization and an end to repression. Along with this came the setting of the sun on the great colonial empires.

In his approach to domestic issues, individual rights and the liberties of colonial subjects, Churchill turned out to be a romantic refugee from a previous era who ended up on the wrong side of history. He did not become Prime Minister, he proclaimed in 1942, "to preside over the liquidation of the British Empire," which then controlled a quarter of the globe's land. But he did. He bulldoggedly opposed the women's rights movement, other civil-rights crusades and decolonization, and he called Mohandas Gandhi "nauseating" and a "half-naked fakir."

As it turned out, Churchill's tenacity was powerful enough to defy Hitler, but not as powerful as the resistance techniques of the half-naked fakir. Gandhi and others who fought for civil rights turned out to be part of a historic tide, one that Roosevelt and his wife Eleanor appreciated better than Churchill did. Which brings us to …

The Century of Civil Rights

IN A CENTURY MARKED by brutality, Mohandas Gandhi perfected a different method of effecting change, one that would turn out (surprisingly) to have more lasting impact. The words he used to describe it do not translate readily into English: Satyagraha (holding firmly onto the deepest truth and soul-force) and ahimsa (the love that remains when all thoughts of violence are dispelled). They formed the basis for civil disobedience and nonviolent resistance. "Nonviolence is the greatest force at the disposal of mankind," he said. "It is mightier than the mightiest weapon of destruction devised by the ingenuity of man."

Part of his creed was that purifying society required purifying one's own soul. "The more you develop nonviolence in your own being, the more infectious it becomes." Or, more pithily: "We must become the change we seek."

He was, truth be told, rather weird at times. His own purification regime involved inordinate attention to the bowel movements of himself and those around him, and he liked testing his powers of self-denial by sleeping naked with young women. Nevertheless, he became not just a political force but a spiritual guide for those repelled by the hate and greed that polluted this century. "Generations to come," said Albert Einstein, "will scarce believe that such a one as this ever in flesh and blood walked upon this earth."

Gandhi's life of civil disobedience began while he was a young lawyer in South Africa when, because he was a dark-skinned Indian, he was told to move to a third-class seat on a train even though he held a first-class ticket. He refused, and ended up spending the night on a desolate platform. It culminated in 1930, when he was 61, and he and his followers marched 240 miles in 24 days to make their own salt from the sea in defiance of British colonial laws. By the time he reached the sea, several thousand had joined his march, and all along the coast thousands more were doing the same. More than 60,000 were eventually arrested, including Gandhi, but it was clear who would end up the victors.

Gandhi did not see the full realization of his dreams; India finally gained independence, but a civil war between Hindus and Muslims resulted, despite his efforts, in partition and the bloody birth of Pakistan. He was killed, on his way to prayers, by a Hindu fanatic. His spirit and philosophy, however, transformed the century. His most notable heir was Martin Luther King Jr. "If humanity is to progress," King once declared, "Gandhi is inescapable."

KING, WHO BEGAN STUDYING GANDHI IN COLLEGE, was initially skeptical about the Mahatma's faith in nonviolence. But by the time of the Montgomery bus boycott, he later wrote, "I had come to see early that the Christian doctrine of love operating through the Gandhian method of nonviolence was one of the most potent weapons available to the Negro in his struggle for freedom." The bus boycott, sit-ins, freedom rides and, above all, the Selma march with its bloody Sunday on the Edmund Pettus Bridge showed how right he (and Gandhi) was.

Civil rights took a variety of forms this century. Women got the right to vote, gained control over their reproductive life and made strides toward achieving equal status in the workplace. Gays and lesbians gained the right to be proud of who they are.

Indeed, one defining aspect of our century has been the degree to which it was shaped not just by powerful political leaders but also by ordinary folks who civilly disobeyed: Nelson Mandela organizing a campaign in 1952 to defy South Africa's "pass laws" by entering white townships, Rosa Parks refusing to give up her seat on a Montgomery bus just as Gandhi had on the South African train, the unknown rebel blocking the line of tanks rumbling toward Tiananmen Square, Lech Walesa leading his fellow Polish workers out on strike, the British suffragist Emmeline Pankhurst launching hunger strikes, American students protesting the Vietnam War by burning their draft cards, and gays and lesbians at Greenwich Village's Stonewall Inn resisting a police raid. In the end, they changed the century as much as the men who commanded armies.

> Nonviolence is the greatest force at the disposal of mankind ... mightier than the mightiest weapon of destruction ...
>
> **MOHANDAS GANDHI**

The Century of Science and Technology

IT IS HARD TO COMPARE THE INFLUENCE OF STATESMEN with that of scientists. Nevertheless, we can note that there are certain eras that were most defined by their politics, others by their culture, and others by their scientific advances. The 18th century, for example, was clearly one marked by statecraft: in 1776 alone there are Thomas Jefferson and Benjamin Franklin writing the Declaration of Independence, Adam Smith publishing *The Wealth of Nations* and George Washington leading the Revolutionary forces. The 17th century, on the other hand, despite such colorful leaders as Louis XIV and the châteaus he left us, will be most remembered for its science: Galileo exploring gravity and the solar system, Descartes developing modern philosophy and Newton discovering the laws of motion and calculus. And the 16th will be remembered for the flourishing of the arts and culture: Michelangelo and Leonardo and Shakespeare creating masterpieces, Elizabeth I inspiring the Elizabethan Age.

So how will the 20th century be remembered? Yes, for democracy. And yes, for civil rights. But the 20th century will be most remembered, like the 17th, for its earthshaking advances in science and technology. In his massive history of the 20th century, Paul Johnson declares, "The scientific genius impinges on humanity, for good or ill, far more than any statesman or warlord." Albert Einstein was more succinct: "Politics is for the moment. An equation is for eternity."

Just look at the year the century was born. The Paris Exposition in 1900 (50 million visitors, more than the entire population of France) featured wireless telegraphs, X rays and tape recorders. "It is a new century, and what we call electricity is its God," wrote the romantic historian Henry Adams from Paris.

In 1900 we began to unlock the mysteries of the atom: Max Planck launched quantum physics by discovering that atoms emit bursts of radiation in packets. Also the mysteries of the mind: Sigmund Freud published *The Interpretation of Dreams* that year. Marconi was preparing to send radio signals across the Atlantic, the Wright Brothers went to Kitty Hawk to work on their gliders, and an unpromising student named Albert Einstein finally graduated, after some difficulty, from college that year. So much for the boneheaded 1899 prediction of Charles Duell, director of the U.S. Patent Office: "Everything that can be invented has been invented."

So many fields of science made such great progress that each could produce its own contender for Person of the Century. Let's start with medicine. In 1928 the young Scottish researcher Alexander Fleming sloppily left a lab dish growing bacteria on a bench when he went on vacation. It got contaminated with a *Penicillium* mold spore; on returning, he noticed that the mold seemed to stop the growth of the germs. His serendipitous discovery would eventually save more lives than were lost in all the century's wars.

Fleming serves well as a symbol of all the great medical researchers, such as Jonas Salk and David Ho, who fought disease. But he personally did little, after his initial eureka! moment, to develop penicillin. Nor has the fight against infectious diseases been so successful that it will stand as a defining achievement of the century.

The century's greater biological breakthrough was more basic. It was unceremoniously announced on Feb. 28, 1953, when Francis Crick winged into the Eagle Pub in Cambridge, England, and declared that he and his partner James Watson had "found the secret of life."

Watson had sketched out how four chemical bases paired to create a self-copying code at the core of the double-helix-shaped DNA molecule. In the more formal announcement of their discovery, a one-page paper in the journal *Nature*, they noted the significance in a famously understated sentence: "It has not escaped our notice that the specific pairing we have postulated immediately suggests a possible copying mechanism for the genetic material." But they were less restrained when persuading Watson's sister to type up the paper for them. "We told her," Watson wrote in *The Double Helix*, "that she was participating in perhaps the most famous event in biology since Darwin's book."

> ## We told her that she was participating in the perhaps the most famous event in biology since [Charles] Darwin's book.
>
> **JAMES WATSON,** in *The Double Helix*

DNA IS LIKELY TO BE THE DISCOVERY MADE IN THE 20th century that will be the most important to the 21st. The world is just a few years away from deciphering the entire sequence of more than 100,000 human genes encoded by the 3 billion chemical pairs of our DNA. That will open the way to new drugs, genetic engineering and designer babies.

So should Watson and Crick be Persons of the Century? Perhaps. But two factors count against them. Their role, unlike that of Einstein or Churchill, would have been performed by others if they hadn't been around; indeed, competitor Linus Pauling was just months away from shouting the same eureka! In addition, although the next century may be, this did not turn out to be a century of genetic engineering.

What about the technologists?

There's Henry Ford, who perfected ways to mass-produce the horseless carriages developed in Germany by Gottlieb Daimler and others. The car became the most influential consumer product of the century, bringing with it a host of effects good and bad: more personal freedom, residential sprawl, social mobility, highways and shopping malls, air pollution (though the end of the noxious pollution produced by horses) and mass markets for mass-produced goods.

The Wright brothers also used the internal-combustion engine to free people from earthly bounds. Their 12-second flight in 1903 transformed both war and peace. As Bill Gates said in his profile for the TIME 100, "Their invention effectively became the World Wide Web of that era, bringing people, languages, ideas and values together." The result was a new era of globalization.

Even more central to this globalization were the electronic technologies that revolutionized the distribution of information, ideas and entertainment. Five centuries ago, Gutenberg's advances in printing helped lead to the Reformation (by permitting people to own their own Bibles and religious tracts), the Renaissance (by permitting ideas to travel from village to village) and the rise of individual liberty (by allowing ordinary folks direct access to information). Likewise, the 20th century was transformed by a string of inventions that, building on the telegraph and telephone of the 19th century, led to a new information age.

In 1927 Philo Farnsworth was able to electronically deconstruct a moving image and transmit it into another room. In the 1930s Alan Turing first described the computer—a machine that could perform logical functions based on whatever instructions were fed to it—and then helped build one in the early 1940s that cracked the German wartime codes. His concepts were refined by other computer pioneers: John von Neumann, John Atanasoff, J. Presper Eckert and John Mauchly.

Meanwhile, another group of scientists—including Enrico Fermi and J. Robert Oppenheimer—was unlocking the power of the atom in a different way, one that led to the creation of a weapon that helped win the war and define the subsequent five decades of nervous peace that ensued.

In 1947 William Shockley and his team at Bell Labs invented the transistor, which had the ability to take an electric current and translate it into on-off binary data. Thus began the digital age. Robert Noyce and Jack Kilby, a decade later, came up with ways to etch many transistors— eventually millions—onto tiny silicon wafers that became known as microchips.

Many people deserve credit for creating the Internet, which began in 1969 as a network of university and military computers and began to take off in 1974 when Vint Cerf and Robert Kahn published a protocol that enabled any computer on the network to transmit to any other. A companion protocol devised by Tim Berners-Lee in 1990 created the World Wide Web, which simplified and popularized navigation on the Net.

The idea that anyone in the world can publish information and have it instantly available to anyone else in the world created a revolution that will rank with Gutenberg's.

Together these triumphs of science and technology advanced the cause of freedom, in some ways more than any statesman or soldier did. In 1989 workers in Warsaw used faxes to spread the word of Solidarity, and schoolkids in Prague slipped into tourist hotels to watch CNN reports on the upheavals in Berlin. A decade later, dissidents in China set up e-mail chains, and Web-surfing students evaded clueless censors to break the government's monopoly on information. Just as the flow of ideas wrought by Gutenberg led to the rise of individual rights, so too did the unfetterable flow of ideas wrought by telephones, faxes, television and the Internet serve as the surest foe of totalitarianism in this century.

Fleming, Watson and Crick, the Wright Brothers, Farnsworth, Turing, Fermi, Oppenheimer, Noyce—any of them could be, conceivably, a justifiable although somewhat narrow choice for Person of the Century. Fortunately, a narrow choice is not necessary.

Person of the Century

IN A CENTURY THAT WILL BE REmembered foremost for its science and technology—in particular for our ability to understand and harness the forces of the atom and the universe—one person stands out as both the greatest mind and paramount icon of our age: the kindly, absentminded professor whose wild halo of hair, piercing eyes, engaging humanity and extrodinary brilliance made his face a symbol and his name a synonym for genius: Albert Einstein.

Slow in learning to talk as a child, expelled by one headmaster and proclaimed by another unlikely to amount to much, Ein-

stein has become the patron saint of distracted schoolkids. But even at age five, he later recalled, he was puzzling over a toy compass and the mysteries of nature's forces.

During his spare time as a young technical officer in a Swiss patent office in 1905, he produced three papers that changed science forever. The first, for which he was later to win the Nobel Prize, described how light could behave not only like a wave but also like a stream of particles, called quanta or photons. This wave-particle duality became the foundation of what is known as quantum physics. It also provided theoretical underpinnings for such 20th century advances as television, lasers and semiconductors. The second paper confirmed the existence of molecules and atoms by statistically showing how their random collisions explained the jerky motion of tiny particles in water.

Important as both these were, it was his third paper that truly upended the universe. It was based, like

much of Einstein's work, on a thought experiment: if you could travel at the speed of light, what would a light wave look like? If you were in a train that neared the speed of light, would you perceive time and space differently?

Einstein's conclusions became known as the special theory of relativity. No matter how fast one is moving toward or away from a source of light, the speed of that light beam will appear the same, a constant 186,000 miles per second. But space and time will appear relative. As a train accelerates to near the speed of light, time on the train will slow down from the vantage point of a stationary observer, and the train will get shorter and heavier. O.K., it's not obvious, but that's why we're no Einstein and he was.

Einstein went on to show that energy and matter were merely different faces of the same thing, their relationship defined by the most famous equation in all of physics: energy equals mass multiplied by the speed of light squared, $E=mc2$. Although not exactly a recipe for an atomic bomb, it explained why one was possible. He also helped resolve smaller mysteries, such as why the sky is blue (it involves how the molecules of air diffuse sunlight).

His crowning glory, perhaps the most beautiful theory in all of science, was the general theory of relativity, published in 1916. Like the special theory, it was based on a thought experiment: imagine being in an enclosed lab accelerating through space. The effects you'd feel would be no different from the experience of gravity. Gravity, he figured, is a warping of space-time. Just as Einstein's earlier work paved the way to harnessing the smallest subatomic forces, the general theory opened up an understanding of the largest of all things, from the formative Big Bang of the universe to its mysterious black holes.

It took three years for astronomers to test this theory by measuring how the sun shifted light coming from a star. The results were announced at a meeting of the Royal Society in London presided over by J.J. Thomson, who in 1897 had discovered the electron. After glancing up at the society's grand portrait of Sir Isaac Newton, Thomson told the assemblage, "Our conceptions of the fabric of the universe must be fundamentally altered." The headline in the next day's *Times* of London read: "Revolution in Science ... Newtonian Ideas Overthrown." The New York *Times* was even more effusive two days later: "Lights All Askew in the Heavens/ Men of Science More or Less Agog Over Results of Eclipse Observations/ Einstein's Theory Triumphs."

EINSTEIN, HITHERTO LITTLE KNOWN, BECAME A global celebrity and was able to sell pictures of himself to journalists and send the money to a charity for war orphans. More than a hundred books were written about relativity within a year.

He also continued his contributions to quantum physics by raising questions that are still playing a pivotal role in the modern development of the theory. Shortly after devising general relativity, he showed that photons have momentum, and he came up with a quantum theory of radiation explaining that all subatomic particles, including electrons, exhibit characteristics of both wave and particle.

This opened the way, alas, to the quantum theories of Werner Heisenberg and others who showed how the wave-particle duality implies a randomness or uncertainty in nature and that particles are affected simply by observing them. This made Einstein uncomfortable. As he famously insisted, "God does not play dice." (Retorted his friendly rival Niels Bohr: "Einstein, stop telling God what to do.") He spent his later years in a failed quest for a unified theory that would explain what appeared to be random or uncertain.

Does Einstein's discomfort with quantum theory make him less a candidate for Person of the Century? Not by much. His own work contributed greatly to quantum theory and to the semiconductor revolution it spawned. And his belief in the existence of a unified field theory could well be proved right in the new century.

More important, he serves as a symbol of all the scientists—such as Heisenberg, Bohr, Richard Feynman and Stephen Hawking, even the ones he disagreed with—who built upon his work to decipher and harness the forces of the cosmos. As James Gleick wrote earlier in the TIME 100 series, "The scientific touchstones of our age—the Bomb, space travel, electronics—all bear his fingerprints." Or, to quote a TIME cover story from 1946: "Among 20th-Century men, he blends to an extraordinary degree those highly distilled powers of intellect, intuition and imagination which are rarely combined in one mind, but which, when they do occur together, men call genius. It was all but inevitable that this genius should appear in the field of science, for 20th-Century civilization is first & foremost technological."

Einstein's theory of relativity not only upended physics, it also jangled the underpinnings of society. For nearly 300 years, the clockwork cosmos of Galileo and Newton—based on absolute laws and certainties—formed the psychological foundation for the Enlightenment, with its belief in causes and effects, order, rationalism, even its emphasis on duty.

Now came a view of the universe in which space and time were all relative. Indirectly, relativity paved the way for a new relativism in morality, arts and politics. There was less faith in absolutes, not only of time and space but also of truth and morality. "It formed a knife," historian Paul Johnson says of relativity theory, "to help cut society adrift from its traditional moorings." Just as Darwinism became, a century ago, not just a biological theory but also a social theology, so too did relativity shape the social theology of the 20th century.

The effect on the arts can be seen by looking at 1922: the year after Einstein won the Nobel Prize, James Joyce published *Ulysses* and T.S. Eliot *The Waste Land*. There was a famous party in May for the debut of the ballet *Renard*, composed by Igor Stravinsky and staged by Sergei Diaghilev. They were both there, along with Pablo Picasso (the set designer), Marcel Proust and Joyce. The art of each, in its own way, reflected the breakdown of mechanical order and of the sense that space and time were absolutes.

In early 1933, as Hitler was taking power, Einstein immigrated to the U.S., settling in Princeton as the world's first scientific supercelebrity. That year he help found a group to resettle refugees, the International Rescue Committee. Thus he became a symbol of another of the great themes of the century: how history was shaped by tides of immigrants, so many of them destined for greatness, who fled oppressive regimes for the freedom of democratic climes.

ROOSEVELT, GANDHI, EINSTEIN. THREE INSPIRING characters, each representing a different force of history in the past century. They were about as different as any three men are likely to be. Yet each in his own way taught us the century's most telling lesson: the value of being both humble and humane.

Roosevelt, scarcely an exemplar of humility, nonetheless saved the possibility of governmental humility from the forces of utopian and dystopian arrogance. Totalitarian systems—fascist or communist—believe the élites know what's best for all. But leaders who nurture democracy and freedom—who allow folks to make their own choices rather than dictating them from on high—are being laudably humble, a stance that the 20th century clearly rewarded and that is necessary for creating humane societies.

Gandhi, unlike Roosevelt, was the earthly embodiment of humility, so much so that at times it threatened to become a conceit. He taught us that we should value the civil liberties and individual rights of other human beings, and he lived for (and was killed for) preaching tolerance and pluralism. By exhibiting these virtues, which the century has amply taught us are essential to civilization, we express the humility and humanity that come from respecting people who are different from us.

Einstein taught the greatest humility of all: that we are but a speck in an unfathomably large universe. The more we gain insight into its mysterious forces, cosmic and atomic, the more reason we have to be humble. And the more we harness the huge power of these forces, the more such humility becomes an imperative. "A spirit is manifest in the laws of the universe," he once wrote, "in the face of which we, with our modest powers, must feel humble."

Einstein often invoked God, although his was a rather depersonalized deity. He believed, he said, in a "God who reveals himself in the harmony of all that exists." His faith in this divine harmony was what caused him to reject the view that the universe is subject to random uncertainty. "The Lord God is subtle, but malicious he is not." Searching for God's design, he said, was "the source of all true art and science." Although this quest may be a cause for humility, it is also what gives meaning and dignity to our lives.

As the century's greatest thinker, as an immigrant who fled from oppression to freedom, as a political idealist, he best embodies what historians will regard as significant about the 20th century. And as a philosopher with faith both in science and in the beauty of God's handiwork, he personifies the legacy that has been bequeathed to the next century.

In a hundred years, as we turn to another new century—nay, ten times a hundred years, when we turn to another new millennium—the name that will prove most enduring from our own amazing era will be that of Albert Einstein: genius, political refugee, humanitarian, locksmith of the mysteries of the atom and the universe. ∎

As a humanist and internationalist, Einstein had spent most of his life espousing a gentle pacifism; he was one of Gandhi's foremost admirers. But in 1939 he signed one of the century's most important letters, one that symbolizes the relationship between science and politics. "It may become possible to set up nuclear chain reactions," he wrote President Roosevelt. "This new phenomenon would also lead to the construction of bombs." When Roosevelt read the letter, he crisply ordered, "This requires action."

TIME *managing editor Walter Isaacson directed the* TIME *100 project. He is the author of* Kissinger: A Biography.

The pre-eminent scientist in a century of science, he placed his stamp on the era's landmarks—the Bomb, the Big Bang, quantum physics and electronics

Albert Ei

(1879-1955)

By **FREDERIC GOLDEN**

PERSON OF THE CENTURY

H e was the embodiment of pure intellect, the bumbling professor with the German accent, a comic cliché in a thousand films. Instantly recognizable, like Charlie Chaplin's Little Tramp, Albert Einstein's shaggy-haired visage was as familiar to ordinary people as to the matrons who fluttered about him in salons from Berlin to Hollywood. Yet he was unfathomably profound—the genius among geniuses who discovered, merely by thinking about it, that the universe was not as it seemed.

Even now scientists marvel at the daring of general relativity ("I still can't see how he thought of it," said the late Richard Feynman, no slouch himself). But the great physicist was also engagingly simple, trading ties and socks for mothy sweaters and sweatshirts. He tossed off pithy aphorisms ("Science is a wonderful thing if one does not have to earn one's living at it") and playful doggerel as easily as equations.

Viewing the hoopla over him with humorous detachment, he variously referred to himself as the Jewish saint or artist's model. He was a cartoonist's dream come true.

Much to his surprise, his ideas, like Darwin's, reverberated beyond science, influencing modern culture from painting to poetry. At first even many scientists didn't really grasp relativity, prompting Arthur Eddington's celebrated wisecrack (asked if it was true that only three people understood relativity, the witty British astrophysicist paused, then said, "I am trying to think who the third person is"). To the

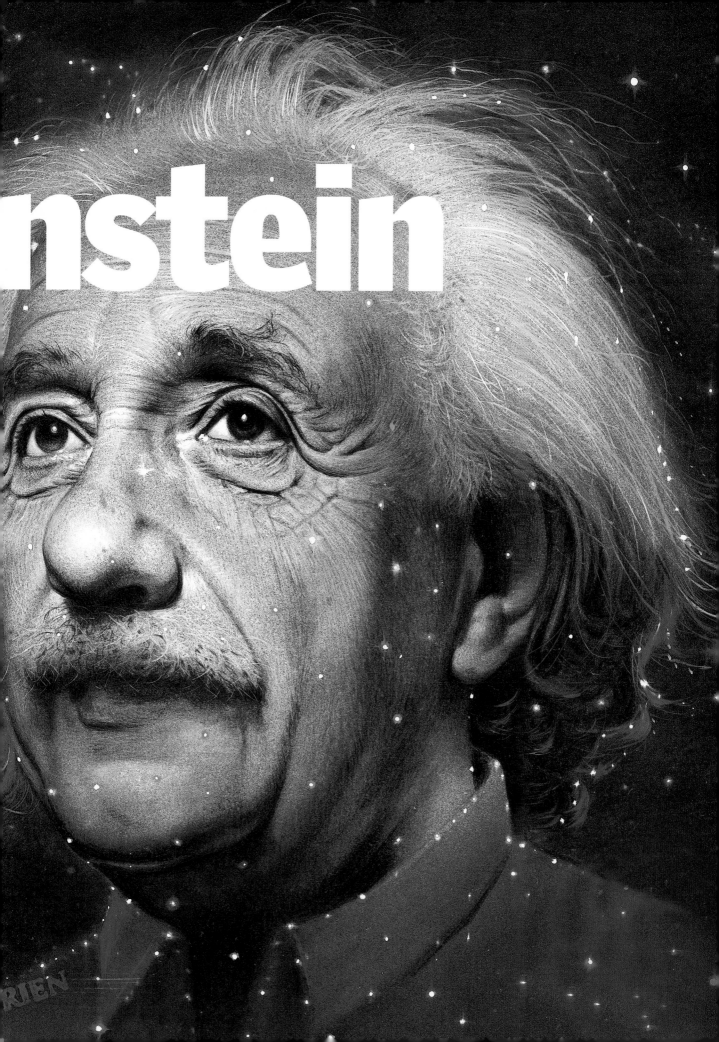

world at large, relativity seemed to pull the rug out from under perceived reality. And for many advanced thinkers of the 1920s, from Dadaists to Cubists to Freudians, that was a fitting credo, reflecting what science historian David Cassidy calls "the incomprehensiveness of the contemporary scene—the fall of monarchies, the upheaval of the social order, indeed, all the turbulence of the 20th century."

EINSTEIN'S GALVANIZING EFFECT ON THE POPULAR imagination continued throughout his life, and after it. Fearful his grave would become a magnet for curiosity seekers, Einstein's executors secretly scattered his ashes. But they were defeated at least in part by a pathologist who carried off his brain in hopes of learning the secrets of his genius. In 1999 Canadian researchers, probing those pickled remains, found that he had an unusually large inferior parietal lobe—a center of mathematical thought and spatial imagery. More definitive insights, though, are emerging from his old letters and papers. These are finally coming to light after years of resistance by executors eager to shield his iconic image.

Unlike the avuncular caricature of his later years who left his hair unshorn, helped little girls with their math homework and was a soft touch for almost any worthy cause, Einstein is emerging from these documents as a man whose unsettled private life contrasts sharply with his serene contemplation of the universe. He could be alternately warmhearted and cold; a doting father, yet aloof; an understanding, if difficult, mate, but also an egregious flirt. "Deeply and passionately [concerned]

Einstein as a young scholar; bicycling in California; with wife Elsa and stepdaughter Margot

with the fate of every stranger," wrote his friend and biographer Philipp Frank, he "immediately withdrew into his shell" when relations became intimate. Einstein himself resisted all efforts to explore his psyche, rejecting, for example, a Freudian analyst's offer to put him on the couch.

The pudgy first child of a bourgeois Jewish couple from southern Germany, he was strongly influenced by his domineering, musically inclined mother, who encouraged his passion for the violin and such classical composers as Bach, Mozart and Schubert. In his preteens he had a brief, intense religious experience, going so far as to chide his assimilated family for eating pork. But this fervor burned itself out, replaced, after he began exploring introductory science texts and his "holy" little geometry book, by a life-long suspicion of all authority.

His easygoing engineer father, an unsuccessful entrepre-

neur in the emerging electrochemical industry, had less influence, though it was he who gave Einstein the celebrated toy compass that inspired his first "thought experiment": what, the five-year-old wondered, made the needle always point north?

At age 15, Einstein staged his first great rebellion. Left behind in Munich when his family moved to northern Italy after another of his father's business failures, he quit his militaristic prep school, renounced his German citizenship and eventually entered the famed Zurich Polytechnic, Switzerland's M.I.T. There he fell in love with a classmate, a Serbian physics student named Mileva Maric. Afflicted with a limp and three years his senior, she was nonetheless a soul mate. He rhapsodized about physics and music with her, called her his Dolly and fathered her illegitimate child—a sickly girl who may have died in infancy or been given up for adoption. They married despite his mother's objections, but the union would not last.

The handsome, irrepressible romantic later complained that Mileva's pathological jealousy was typical of women of such "uncommon ugliness." Perhaps remorseful about the lost child and distanced by Einstein's absorption with his work—his only real passion—and his growing fame, Mileva became increasingly unhappy. On the eve of World War I, she reluctantly accompanied Einstein to Berlin, the citadel of European physics, but found the atmosphere insufferable and soon returned to Zurich with their two sons.

By 1919, after three years of long-distance wrangling, they divorced. Still, they continued to have contact, mostly having to do with their sons. The elder, Hans Albert, would become a distinguished professor of hydraulics at the University of California, Berkeley (and, like his father, a passionate sailor). The younger, Eduard, gifted in music and literature, would die in a Swiss psychiatric hospital. Mileva helped support herself by tutoring in mathematics and physics. Despite speculation about her possible unacknowl-

> ## Science is a wonderful thing if one does not have to earn one's living at it.
>
> **ALBERT EINSTEIN**

edged contributions to her husband's work on special relativity, she herself never made such claims.

Einstein, meanwhile, had taken up with a divorced cousin, Elsa, who jovially cooked and cared for him during the emotionally draining months when he made the intellectual leaps that finally resulted in general relativity. Unlike Mileva, she gave him personal space, and not just for science. As he became more widely known, women swarmed around him like moonlets circling a planet. The resulting dalliances irritated Elsa, who eventually became his wife, but as she told a friend, a genius of her husband's kind could never be irreproachable in every respect.

Cavalier as he may have been about his wives, he had a deep moral sense. At the height of World War I, he risked the Kaiser's wrath by signing an antiwar petition, one of only four scientists in Germany to do so. Yet, paradoxically, he helped develop a gyrocompass for U-boats. During the troubled 1920s, when Jews were being singled out by Hitler's rising Nazi Party as the cause of Germany's defeat and economic woes, Einstein and his "Jewish physics" were

a favorite target. Nazis, however, weren't his only foes. For Stalinists, relativity represented rampant capitalist individualism; for some churchmen, it meant ungodly atheism, even though Einstein, who had an impersonal Spinozan view of God, often spoke about trying to understand how the Lord (*der Alte*, or the Old Man) shaped the universe.

In response to Germany's growing anti-Semitism, he became a passionate Zionist, yet he also expressed concern about the rights of Arabs in any Jewish state. Forced to quit Germany when the Nazis came to power, Einstein accepted an appointment at the new Institute for Advanced Study in Princeton, N.J., a scholarly retreat largely created around him. (Asked what he thought he should be paid, Einstein, a financial innocent, suggested $3,000 a year. Hardheaded Elsa got that upped to $16,000.) Though occupied with his lonely struggle to unify gravity and electromagnetism in a single mathematical framework, he watched Germany's furious saber rattling with alarm. Despite his earlier pacifism, he spoke in favor of military action against Hitler. Without fanfare, he helped bring scores of Jewish refugees into a suspicious U.S.

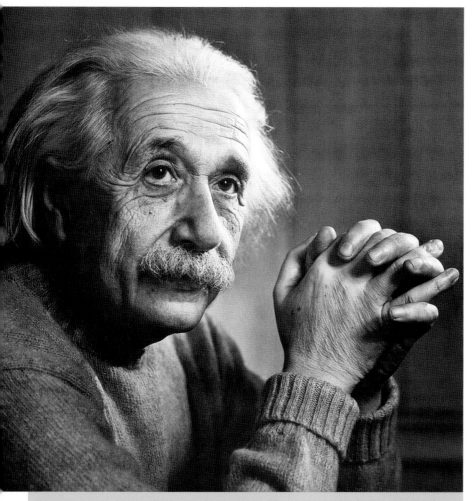

Posing in grand old age; the famous halo of hair suggested both sanctity and intellect

Alerted by the émigré Hungarian scientist Leo Szilard to the possibility that the Germans might build an atom bomb, he wrote F.D.R. of the danger, even though he knew little about recent developments in nuclear physics. When Szilard told Einstein about chain reactions, he was astonished: "I never thought about that at all," he said. Later, when he learned of the destruction of Hiroshima and Nagasaki, he uttered a pained sigh.

Following World War II, Einstein became even more outspoken. Besides campaigning for a ban on nuclear weaponry, he denounced McCarthyism and pleaded for an end to bigotry and racism. Coming as they did at the height of the cold war, the haloed professor's words seemed well meaning if naive; LIFE magazine listed Einstein as one of this country's 50 prominent "dupes and fellow travelers." Harvard physicist and historian Gerald Holton notes, "If Einstein's ideas are really naive, the world is in pretty bad shape." Rather, it seems to him that Einstein's humane and democratic instincts are "an ideal political model for the 21st century." What more could we ask of a man we choose to personify the past 100 years? ∎

A Brief History of Relativity

What is it? How does it work? Why does it change everything? A primer by the most esteemed living physicist

By STEPHEN HAWKING

TOWARD THE END OF THE 19TH CENTURY SCIENTISTS BELIEVED they were close to a complete description of the universe. They imagined that space was filled everywhere by a continuous medium called the ether. Light rays and radio signals were waves in this ether just as sound is pressure waves in air. All that was needed to complete the theory was careful measurements of the elastic properties of the ether; once they had those nailed down, everything else would fall into place.

Soon, however, discrepancies with the idea of an all-pervading ether began to appear. You would expect light to travel at a fixed speed through the ether. So if you were traveling in the same direction as the light, you would expect that its speed would appear to be lower, and if you were traveling in the opposite direction to the light, that its speed would appear to be higher. Yet a series of experiments failed to find any evidence for differences in speed due to motion through the ether.

The most careful and accurate of these experiments was carried out by Albert Michelson and Edward Morley at the Case Institute in Cleveland, Ohio, in 1887. They compared the speed of light in two beams at right angles to each other. As the earth rotates on its axis and orbits the sun, they reasoned, it will move through the ether, and the speed of light in these two beams should diverge. But the two men found no daily or yearly differences between the two beams of light. It was as if light always traveled at the same speed relative to you, no matter how you were moving.

The Irish physicist George FitzGerald and the Dutch physicist Hendrik Lorentz were the first to suggest that bodies moving through the ether would contract and that clocks would slow. This shrinking and slowing would be such that everyone would measure the same speed for light no matter how they were moving with respect to the ether, which FitzGerald and Lorentz regarded as a real substance.

But it was a young clerk named Albert Einstein, working in the Swiss Patent Office in Bern, who cut through the ether and solved the speed-of-light problem once and for all. In June 1905 he wrote one of three papers that would establish him as one of the world's leading theoretical scientists—and in the process start two conceptual revolutions that changed our understanding of time, space and reality.

His theory confirmed,
Einstein went to Paris
in 1922 to explain it

In that 1905 paper, Einstein pointed out that because you could not detect whether or not you were moving through the ether, the whole notion of an ether was redundant. Instead, Einstein started from the postulate that the laws of science should appear the same to all freely moving observers. In particular, observers should all measure the same speed for light no matter how they were moving.

This required abandoning the idea that there is a universal quantity called time that all clocks measure. Instead, everyone would have his own personal time. The clocks of two people would agree if they were at rest with respect to each other but not if they were moving. This has been confirmed by a number of experiments, including one in which an extremely accurate timepiece was flown around the world and then compared with one that had stayed in place.

If you wanted to live longer, in theory you could keep flying to the east so the speed of the plane added to the earth's rotation. (However, the tiny fraction of a second you gained would be more than offset by eating airline meals.)

Einstein's postulate that the laws of nature should appear the same to all freely moving observers was the foundation of the theory of relativity, so called because it implies that only relative motion is important. Its beauty and simplicity were convincing to many scientists and philosophers. But there remained a lot of opposition. Einstein had overthrown two of the Absolutes (with a capital A) of 19th century science: Absolute Rest, which was represented by the ether, and Absolute or Universal Time, which all clocks measured. Did this imply, people asked, that there were no absolute moral standards, that everything was relative?

Special Relativity

Einstein's 1905 theory claims that light moves through a vacuum at a constant speed relative to any observer, no matter what the observer's motion—with bizarre consequences

Relativity and Time

A moving clock runs slower than a stationary one from the perspective of a stationary observer

1 A man riding a moving train is timing a light beam that travels from ceiling to floor and back again. From his point of view, the light moves straight down and straight up.

— Light

Distance light pulse travels

The observer riding the train thinks the light bulb and mirror are standing still

— Mirror

2 From trackside, Einstein sees man, bulb and mirror moving sideways: the light traces a diagonal path. From Einstein's viewpoint, the light goes farther. But since lightspeed is always the same, the event must take more time by his clock.

Distance light pulse travels, as seen by Einstein, is farther

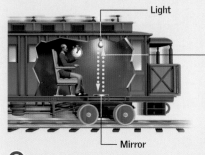

The observer watching the train thinks the light bulb and mirror are moving

More time has elapsed

Relativity and Length

A moving object appears to shrink in the direction of motion, as seen by a stationary observer

1 The man now observes a light beam that travels the length of the train car. Knowing the speed of light and the travel time of the light beam, he can calculate the length of the train.

Distance light pulse travels, as seen by observer on train

The observer on the train sees only the motion of the light beam

2 Einstein is not moving, so the rear of the train is moving forward from his point of view to meet the beam of light: for him the beam travels a shorter distance. Because the speed of light is always the same, he will calculate the train's length as shorter— even after he allows for his faster-ticking clock. As the train approaches the speed of light, its length shrinks to nearly zero.

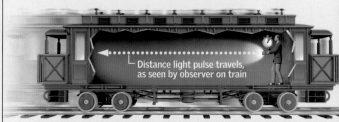

Distance light pulse travels, as seen by Einstein

Someone watching from outside sees the light beam moving but with the motion of the train added

Sources: *World Book Encyclopedia; Einstein for Beginners*

Politics is for the moment, while ...an equation is for eternity.

ALBERT EINSTEIN

This unease continued through the 1920s and '30s. When Einstein was awarded the Nobel Prize in 1921, the citation was for important—but by Einstein's standards comparatively minor—work also carried out in 1905. There was no mention of relativity, which was considered too controversial. (I still get two or three letters a week telling me Einstein was wrong. Nevertheless, the theory of relativity is now completely accepted by the scientific community, and its predictions have been verified in countless applications.)

A very important consequence of relativity is the relation between mass and energy. Einstein's postulate that the speed of light should appear the same to everyone implied that nothing could be moving faster than light. What happens is that as energy is used to accelerate a particle or a spaceship, the object's mass increases, making it harder to accelerate further. To accelerate the particle to the speed of light is impossible because it would take an infinite amount of energy. The equivalence of mass and energy is summed up in Einstein's famous equation $E=mc^2$, probably the only physics equation to enjoy recognition on the street.

Among the consequences of this law is that if the nucleus of a uranium atom fissions (splits) into two nuclei with slightly less total mass, a tremendous amount of energy is released. Einstein's 1939 letter to President Roosevelt urging the U.S. to start a program of nuclear research led to the Manhattan Project and the atom bomb that exploded over Hiroshima in 1945. Some people still blame the atom bomb on Einstein because he discovered the relation between mass and energy. But that's like blaming Newton for the gravity that causes airplanes to crash. Einstein took no part

General Relativity

In 1915 Einstein broadened his special theory of relativity to include gravity. In general relativity, light always takes the shortest possible route from one point to another

The Equivalence of Gravity and Acceleration

Without external clues, it's impossible to tell if you're being pulled downward by gravity or accelerating upward. Your legs will feel the same pressure; a ball will fall precisely the same way

The realization that gravity and acceleration are equivalent was a key insight that eventually allowed Einstein to construct his theory of general relativity.

Relativity and Gravity

According to relativity, gravity is not a force; it's a warping of space-time (which is an amalgam of time and space) that happens in the presence of mass. The warping is analogous to tbe bending of a rubber sheet when a weight is placed on it

1 When starlight passes near a massive body, such as the sun, the shortest route is a curved line that follows the curvature of space-time. Thus, the starlight appears to be coming from a different point than its actual origin. The observation of this effect in 1919 convinced physicists that Einstein's strange theory was right.

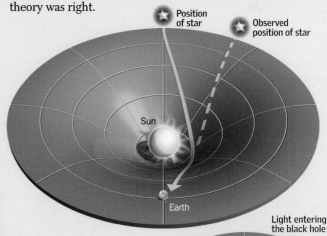

Position of star

Observed position of star

Sun

Earth

Light entering the black hole

2 If a mass is concentrated enough, the curvature of space-time becomes infinite. This phenomenon is known as a black hole because a light beam that comes too close will never escape.

TIME Graphics by Ed Gabel and Joe Lertola

LOTTE JACOBI ARCHIVE—UNIVERSITY OF NEW HAMPSHIRE

Why '100 Authors Against Einstein'? If I were wrong, one would have been enough.

ALBERT EINSTEIN, on the Nazis' publication of a book opposing relativity

in the Manhattan Project and was horrified by the explosion.

Although the theory of relativity fit well with the laws that govern electricity and magnetism, it wasn't compatible with Newton's law of gravity. This law said that if you changed the distribution of matter in one region of space, the change in the gravitational field would be felt instantaneously everywhere else in the universe. Not only would this mean you could send signals faster than light (something that was forbidden by relativity), but it also required the Absolute, or Universal, Time that relativity had abolished in favor of personal, or relativistic, time.

EINSTEIN WAS AWARE OF THIS DIFFICULTY IN 1907, while he was still at the patent office in Bern, but didn't begin to think seriously about the problem until he was at the German University in Prague in 1911. He realized that there is a close relationship between acceleration and a gravitational field. Someone in a closed box cannot tell whether he is sitting at rest in the earth's gravitational field or being accelerated by a rocket in free space. (This being before the age of *Star Trek*, Einstein thought of people in elevators rather than spaceships. But you cannot accelerate or fall freely very far in an elevator before disaster strikes.)

If the earth were flat, one could equally well say that the apple fell on Newton's head because of gravity or that Newton's head hit the apple because he and the surface of the earth were accelerating upward. This equivalence between acceleration and gravity didn't seem to work for a round earth, however; people on the other side of the world would have to be accelerating in the opposite direction but staying at a constant distance from us.

On his return to Zurich in 1912 Einstein had a brainstorm. He realized that the equivalence of gravity and acceleration could work if there was some give-and-take in the geometry of reality. What if space-time—an entity Einstein

Einstein fled the Nazis, becoming an American citizen in 1940

invented to incorporate the three familiar dimensions of space with a fourth dimension, time—was curved, and not flat, as had been assumed? If so, mass and energy would warp space-time in some manner yet to be determined. Objects like apples or planets would try to move in straight lines through space-time, but their paths would appear to be bent by a gravitational field because space-time is curved.

With the help of his friend Marcel Grossmann, Einstein studied the theory of curved spaces and surfaces that had been developed by Bernhard Riemann as a piece of abstract mathematics, without any thought that it would be relevant to the real world. In 1913, Einstein and Grossmann wrote a paper in which they put forward the idea that what we think of as gravitational forces is just an expression of the fact that space-time is curved. However, because of a mistake by Einstein (who was quite human and fallible), they weren't able to find the equations that related the curvature of space-time to the mass and energy in it.

Einstein continued to work on the problem in Berlin, undisturbed by domestic matters and largely unaffected by the war, until he finally found the right equations, in November 1915. Einstein had discussed his ideas with the mathematician David Hilbert during a visit to the University of Göttingen in the summer of 1915, and Hilbert independently found the same equations a few days before Einstein. Nevertheless, as Hilbert admitted, the credit for the new theory belonged to Einstein. It was his idea to relate gravity to the warping of space-time. It is a tribute to the civilized state of Germany in this period that such scientific discussions and exchanges could go on undisturbed even in wartime. What a contrast to 20 years later!

The new theory of curved space-time was called general relativity to distinguish it from the original theory without gravity, which was now known as special relativity. It was confirmed in spectacular fashion in 1919, when a British expedition to West Africa observed a slight shift in the position of stars near the sun during an eclipse. Their light, as Einstein had predicted, was bent as it passed the sun. Here was direct evidence that space and time are warped, the greatest change in our perception of the arena in which we live since Euclid wrote his *Elements* about 300 B.C.

Einstein's general theory of relativity transformed space and time from a passive background in which events take place to active participants in the dynamics of the cosmos. This led to a great problem that is still at the forefront of physics at the end of the 20th century. The universe is full of matter, and matter warps space-time so that bodies fall together. Einstein found that his equations didn't have a solution that described a universe that was unchanging in time. Rather than give up a static and everlasting universe, which he and most other people believed in at that time, he fudged the equations by adding a term called the cosmological constant, which warped space-time the other way so that bodies move apart, thus balancing the attractive effect of matter and allowing for a universe that lasts for all time.

This was one of the great missed opportunities of theo-

Einstein pays a visit to the observatory at Mount Wilson, where the Big Bang was discovered

that hold at all other times. We have made some progress toward this goal, but we don't yet have a complete understanding of the origin of the universe.

The reason general relativity broke down at the Big Bang was that it was not compatible with quantum theory, the other great conceptual revolution of the early 20th century. The first step toward quantum theory came in 1900, when Max Planck, working in Berlin, discovered that the radiation from a body that was glowing red hot could be explained if light came only in packets of a certain size, called quanta. In one of his groundbreaking 1905 papers, Einstein showed that Planck's quantum hypothesis could explain what is called the photoelectric effect, the way certain metals give off electrons when light falls on them. The basis of modern light detectors and television cameras, this work earned Einstein the 1921 Nobel Prize in Physics.

Einstein continued to work on the quantum idea into the 1920s but was deeply disturbed by the work of Werner Heisenberg in Copenhagen, Paul Dirac in Cambridge and Erwin Schrödinger in Zurich, who developed a new picture of reality called quantum mechanics. No longer did tiny particles have a definite position and speed. On the contrary, the more accurately you determined the particle's position, the less accurately you could determine its speed, and vice versa.

Einstein was horrified by this random, unpredictable element in the basic laws and never fully accepted quantum mechanics. His feelings were expressed in his famous God-does-not-play-dice dictum. Most other scientists, however, accepted the validity of the new quantum laws because they showed excellent agreement with observations and because they seemed to explain a whole range of phenomena previously unaccounted for. They are the basis of the developments in chemistry, molecular biology and electronics that have transformed the world in the past half-century.

retical physics. If Einstein had stuck with his original equations, he could have predicted that the universe must be either expanding or contracting. As it was, the possibility of a time-dependent universe wasn't taken seriously until observations made in the 1920s with the 100-in. telescope on Mount Wilson revealed that the farther other galaxies are from us, the faster they are moving away. In other words, the universe is expanding and the distance between any two galaxies is steadily increasing with time. Einstein later called the cosmological constant his greatest mistake.

G ENERAL RELATIVITY COMPLETELY CHANGED THE discussion of the origin and fate of the universe. A static universe could have existed forever or could have been created in its present form at some time in the past. On the other hand, if galaxies are moving apart today, they must have been closer together in the past. About 15 billion years ago, they would all have been on top of one another and their density would have been infinite. According to the general theory, this Big Bang was the beginning of the universe and of time itself. So maybe Einstein deserves to be the person of a longer period than just the past 100 years.

General relativity also predicts that time comes to a stop inside black holes, regions of space-time that are so warped that light cannot escape them. But both the beginning and the end of time are places where the equations of general relativity fall apart. Thus the theory cannot predict what should emerge from the Big Bang. Some see this as an indication of God's freedom to start the universe off any way God wanted. Others (myself included) feel that the beginning of the universe should be governed by the same laws

The equations of general relativity are Einstein's best epitaph and memorial. They should last as long as the universe. The world has changed far more in the past 100 years than in any other century in history. The reason is not political or economic but technological—technologies that flowed directly from advances in basic science. Clearly, no scientist better represents those advances than Albert Einstein, TIME's Person of the Century. ■

Professor Hawking, author of A Brief History of Time, *holds the Cambridge University chair once held by Isaac Newton.*

Unfinished Symphony

Strings may finally do what Einstein failed to do: tie together the two great irreconcilable ideas of 20th century physics

By J. MADELEINE NASH

I AM GENERALLY REGARDED AS A SORT OF PETRI-fied object, rendered deaf and blind by the years," Albert Einstein confided near the end of his life. He was, alas, correct. During the last three decades of his remarkable career, Einstein had become obsessed by the dream of producing a unified field theory, a series of equations that would establish an underlying link between the seemingly unrelated forces of gravity and electromagnetism.

In so doing, Einstein hoped also to resolve the conflict between two competing visions of the universe: the smooth continuum of space-time, where stars and planets reign, as described by his general theory of relativity, and the unseemly jitteriness of the submicroscopic quantum world, where particles hold sway.

Einstein worked hard on the problem, but success eluded him. That didn't surprise his contemporaries, who saw his quest as a quixotic indulgence. They were sure that the greatest of all their colleagues was simply wasting his time, relying on a conceptual approach that was precisely backward. In contrast to just about all other physicists, Einstein was convinced that in the conflict between quantum mechanics and general relativity, it was the former that constituted the crux of the problem. "I must seem like an ostrich who forever buries its head in the relativistic sand in order not to face the evil quanta," Einstein reflected in 1954.

We know now, however, that it is Einstein's theory that ultimately fails. On extremely fine scales, space-time, and thus reality itself, becomes grainy and discontinuous, like a badly overmagnified newspaper photograph. The equations of general relativity simply can't handle such a situation, where the laws of cause and effect break down and particles jump from point A to point B without going through the space in between. In such a world, you can only calculate what will probably happen next—which is just what quantum theory is designed to do.

Einstein could never accept that the universe was at its heart a cosmic crapshoot, so that today his papers on the unified field theory seem hopelessly archaic. But the puzzle they tried to solve is utterly fundamental. In fact, Einstein's recognition of the problem was so far-sighted that only now has a new generation of physicists caught up and at last taken on the challenge of creating a complete theory—one capable of explaining, in Einstein's words, "every element of the physical reality." And judging from the progress they have made, the next century could usher in an intellectual revolution even more exciting than the one Einstein helped launch in the early 1900s.

Already, in fact, theoretical physicists have succeeded in building a framework that offers the best hope yet of integrating gravity with nature's other fundamental forces. This framework is popularly known as string theory because it postulates that the smallest, indivisible components of the universe are not point-like particles but infinitesimal loops that resemble tiny vibrating strings. "String theory," theorist Edward Witten of Einstein's own Institute for Advanced Study has observed, "is a piece of 21st century physics that fell by chance into the 20th century."

The trouble is, no one knows how many other pieces must fall into place before scientists succeed in solving this greatest of all puzzles. One major reason, observes Columbia University physicist Brian Greene, is that string theory developed backward. "In most theories, physicists first see an overarching idea and then put equations to it." In string theory, says Greene, "we're still trying to figure out the central nugget of truth."

String theory enjoyed a brief vogue in the early 1970s, but then most physicists stopped working on it. Theorist John Schwarz of Caltech and his colleague Joel Scherk of the Ecole Normale Supérieure, however, persevered, and in 1974 their patience was rewarded. For some time they had noticed that some of the vibrating strings spilling out of their equations didn't correspond to the particles they had expected. At first they viewed these mathematical apparitions as nuisances. Then they looked at them more closely; the ghosts that haunted their equations, they decided, were gravitons, the still hypothetical particles that are believed to carry the gravitational force.

Einstein at work in his Princeton study, 1939

Replacing particles with strings eliminated at least one problem that had bedeviled scientists trying to meld general relativity and quantum mechanics. This difficulty arose because space lacks smoothness below subatomic scales. When distances become unimaginably small, space bubbles and churns frenetically, an effect sometimes referred to as quantum foam. Pointlike particles, including the graviton, are likely to be tossed about by quantum foam, like Lilliputian boats to which ripples in the ocean loom as large waves. Strings, by contrast, are miniature ocean liners whose greater size lets them span many waves at once, making them impervious to such disturbances.

Nature rarely bestows gifts on scientists, however, without exacting a price. In this case, the price takes the form of additional complications. Among other things, string theory requires the existence of up to seven dimensions in addition to the by now familiar four (height, width, length and time). It also requires the existence of an entirely new class of subatomic particles, known as supersymmetric particles, or "sparticles." Moreover, there isn't just one string theory but five. Although scientists could rule out none of them, it seemed impossible that all of them could be right.

But that has indeed turned out to be the case. In 1995, Witten, perhaps the most brilliant theorist working in physics today, declared that all five supersymmetric string theories represented different approximations of a deeper, underlying theory. He called it M theory. The insight electrified his colleagues and inspired a flurry of productive activity that has now convinced many that string theory is, in fact, on the right track. "It smells right and it feels right," declares Caltech's Kip Thorne, an expert on black holes and general relativity. "At this early stage in the development of a theory, you have to go on smell and feel."

The M in M theory stands for many things, says Witten, including matrix, mystery and magic. But now he has added murky to the list. Why? Not even Witten, it turns out, has been able to write down the full set of mathematical equations that describe exactly what M theory is, for it has added still more layers of complexity to an already enormous problem. Witten appears reconciled to the possibility that decades may pass before M matures into a theory with real predictive power. "It's like when you're hiking in the mountains," he muses, "and occasionally you reach the top of a pass and get a completely new view. You enjoy the view for a bit, until eventually the truth sinks in. You're still a long way from your destination."

a world made of string ...

Matter is composed of atoms ...

Atoms are made of protons, neutrons and electrons ...

Electrons can't be divided further, but protons and neutrons are each made of three even tinier particles called quarks ...

Now it appears that quarks and electrons may not be particles at all but multi-dimensional entities called "branes," some of which manifest themselves as tiny loops of "string"

> String theory is a piece of 21st century physics
> that fell by chance into the 20th century.
>
> **EDWARD WITTEN, theoretical physicist**

Einstein was brilliant, but he was also lucky. When he developed the general theory of relativity, he dealt with a world that had just three spatial dimensions plus time. As a result, he could use off-the-shelf mathematics to solve his equations. M theorists can't: their science resides in an 11-dimensional world that is filled with weird objects called branes. Strings, in this nomenclature, are one-dimensional branes; membranes are two-dimensional branes. But there are also higher-dimensional branes that no one, including Witten, quite knows how to deal with. For these branes can fold and curl into any number of bewildering shapes.

Which shapes represent the fundamental structures in our universe? On this point, string theorists are currently clueless. For the world conjured into existence by M theory is so exotic that scientists are being forced to work not just at the frontier of physics but at the frontier of mathematics as well. Indeed, it may be that they lack some absolutely essential tool and will have to develop it, just as Isaac Newton was pushed by his investigations of the laws of motion to develop the calculus. As if that weren't hard enough, there is yet another major impediment to progress: unlike quantum mechanics, string theory and its offshoots have developed in the virtual absence of experimental evidence that could help steer theorists in productive directions. Over the next decade, this situation could change. Hopes are running high that upcoming experiments at giant particle colliders in the U.S. and Europe will provide the first tantalizing glimpses of supersymmetry. More speculatively, these experiments could also detect the first subtle signs of additional dimensions.

What would Einstein have made of such wild imaginings? Columbia's Greene, for one, thinks the great theorist would have loved them. After all, Greene notes in his book, *The Elegant Universe*, Einstein played around with the idea of extra dimensions as a strategy for producing a unified field theory. In fact, Greene believes a young Einstein, starting his professional career now rather than at the turn of the past century, would have overcome his deep distrust of quantum mechanics and enthusiastically embraced branes and sparticles and superstrings. And given his almost superhuman ability to transcend conventional thinking and visualize the world in unprecedented ways, he might have been the one to crack the ultimate theory. It may take another Einstein to complete Einstein's unfinished intellectual symphony. ∎

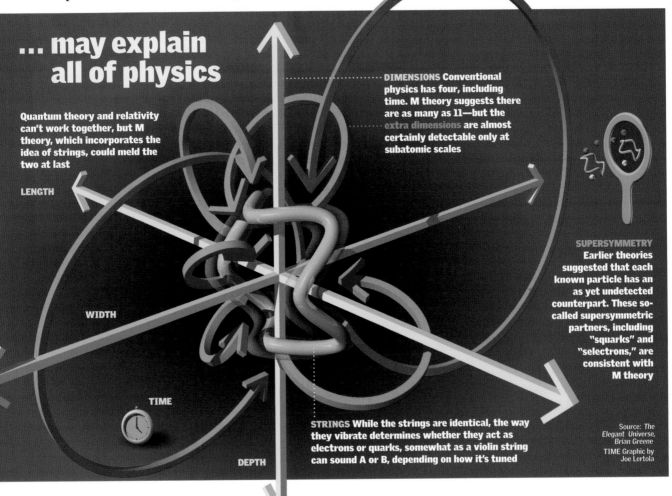

... may explain all of physics

Quantum theory and relativity can't work together, but M theory, which incorporates the idea of strings, could meld the two at last

LENGTH

WIDTH

TIME

DEPTH

DIMENSIONS Conventional physics has four, including time. M theory suggests there are as many as 11—but the extra dimensions are almost certainly detectable only at subatomic scales

SUPERSYMMETRY Earlier theories suggested that each known particle has an as yet undetected counterpart. These so-called supersymmetric partners, including "squarks" and "selectrons," are consistent with M theory

STRINGS While the strings are identical, the way they vibrate determines whether they act as electrons or quarks, somewhat as a violin string can sound A or B, depending on how it's tuned

Source: *The Elegant Universe*, Brian Greene

TIME Graphic by Joe Lertola

The Age of Einstein

He became, almost despite himself, the emblem of all that was new, original and unsettling in the modern age

By ROGER ROSENBLATT

FOR ALBERT EINSTEIN TO BECOME A MODern icon, especially in America, required a total revision of the definition of a hero, since anti-intellectualism has been an integral part of our culture. Here it is not enough to be smart; one must compensate for one's intelligence by also showing the canniness and real-world power of the cowboy and the pioneer. Einstein did this. He was the first modern intellectual superstar, and he won his stardom in the only manner that Americans could accept—by dint of intuitive, not scholarly, intelligence and by having his thought applied to practical things, such as rockets and atom bombs.

The recognition of the practical power of his ideas coincided with a time when such power was most needed. Einstein came to America in 1933 as the most celebrated of a distinguished group of European intellectuals, refugees from Hitler and Mussolini, who quickly changed the composition of both university faculties and government. Until F.D.R.'s New Deal, the country had never associated the contemplative life with governmental action. Now there was a Brain Trust; being an "egghead" was useful, admirable, even sexy. One saw that it was possible to out-think the enemy. Einstein wrote a letter to Roosevelt urging the making of a uranium bomb, and soon a coterie of can-do intellectuals convened at Los Alamos to become the new cowboys of war machinery. Presidents have relied on eggheads ever since: Einstein begat Kissinger begat Rubin and Greenspan.

As for the appeal of his intuitive imagination, it helped that Einstein was initially not associated with a brand-name institution of higher learning, and that his stature did not depend on official accreditation—both of which Americans at once insist on and do not trust. To the contrary: he was eagerly adopted by ordinary folks, though he spoke the obscure language of mathematics, because he seemed removed from snooty trappings. In fact, he seemed removed from the planet, to be out of things in the way the public often adores: a lovable dreamer.

So strong was the image he created that he affected both

A prisoner of fame, Einstein once listed his occupation as "artist's model"

culture and politics in ways that were sometimes wholly opposite to his beliefs and intentions. That his theory of relativity was readily mistranslated as a justification for relativism says more about the way the world was already tending than about Einstein. His stature gave an underpinning to ideas that had nothing to do with his science or personal inclinations. The entire thrust of modern art, whether it took the form of Expressionism, Cubism, Fauvism or fantasy, was a conscious effort to rejigger the shapes of observable reality in the same spirit of liberation and experimentation that Einstein brought to science.

But relativism—that is, the idea that moral and ethical truth exists in the point of view of the beholder—owed nothing to Einstein (who believed the opposite), except a generalized homage to revolutionary thought. Art's elimination of semblances to the physical world corresponded vaguely with Einstein's way of seeing time and space, but it really sprung from an atmosphere of change, in which Einstein was yoked with Freud, Marx, Picasso, Bergson, Wittgenstein, Joyce, Kafka, Duchamp, Kandinsky and anyone else with original and disruptive ideas and an aggressive sense of the new. By that tenuous connection did the discoverer of relativity become a major figure of a world consisting of individuals interpreting the world individually. He was similarly associated with the pluralism of modern music and the eclecticism of modern architecture. In literature, things were ready to fall apart on their own: in 1919 relativity exploded upon science. In 1922 T.S. Eliot's *The Waste Land* had a similar effect on literature. Yet when Eliot wrote, "these fragments I have shored against my ruins," people took up the fragments but ignored the shoring.

The key, though, in Eliot and other 20th century writers, lay in the prominence of the pronoun I—the center of relativistic thought. Thus spake the confessional poetry of the 1960s, the memoirs of the '80s and '90s, the prominence of the narrator in all of modern fiction. A commonplace paradox soon characterized fiction: the antihero, who was disempowered by modern bureaucracies and machines, was simultaneously exalted by his diminished status.

RELATIVISM BROUGHT THE UNDERGROUND MAN into his own—in Europe, with Dostoyevsky, Kafka, Beckett, Sartre, Mann and Pirandello; in America with Fitzgerald, Hemingway, Ellison, Capote and Salinger. The antihero, too, searched for unified meaning, but the narrative that held him was all about divisions, schisms and self-inspection. He sought to be by himself, like a god. In Robert Musil's *The Man Without Qualities* and Richard Wright's *The Outsider*, protagonists become serial killers out of the desire to be alone.

All this has nothing to do with relativity, but it had much to do with Einstein's contemplation of relativity. Einstein became the emblem not only of the desire to know the truth but also of the capacity to know the truth. What this view did for politics involved pure destruction. Paul Johnson connects relativism to the extreme nationalism of 20th century political movements in his generally persuasive view of *Modern Times*. The relationship he cites is sometimes elliptical. What one can say is that the destruction of absolutes—monarchies no less than Newtonian physics—created a vacuum, and in certain key places that vacuum was filled by maniacs and murderers.

There is a connection, though, between European Romanticism, which came into being at the tail end of the 18th century, and the totalitarian credos that bloomed like sudden deadly plants in the first third of the 20th. Einstein did not promote the image of man at the center of the cosmos, controlling the stars by thought. But, quite by accident, he was that image. Merely by being, he corroborated

By now an icon, Einstein plays the clown on his 72nd birthday

the Romantic view that people were 10 feet tall, capable of knowing heaven, and, in the Byronic mode, of speaking directly to God. The logical consequence of such "thinking" was that some people were more able to speak to God than were others, and that God, in turn, spoke to a selected few. Throw in social Darwinism, and by the time the 20th century was under way, Romanticism led directly to Dachau, Auschwitz, the Gulags, the hills of skulls in Cambodia and most recently the fields of graves in Bosnia.

Einstein's essays in *Out of My Later Years* reveal that he held none of the artistic or political ideas that some extrapolated from his work. Whatever revisions he made of Newton, he continued to side with his predecessor on the issue of causality. He abhorred chaos and revolution for its own sake. He was devoted to constancy as much as to relativity, and to the illogical and the senses. In the end, his most useful gift may be not that he pulled the world apart but that once that was done, he strove to put it back together.

Why, finally, is he so important to the age? Not because he personified brainpower—not because he was "an Einstein"—but rather because he demonstrated that the imagination is capable of coming to terms with experience. Simply by gazing into existence, he concluded that time and space could be warped, that mass and energy were interchangeable. He understood that the world was a puzzle created for deciphering and, more, that a person's place in the order of things was to solve as much of the puzzle as possible. This is what makes a human human; this, and the governing elements of morals and humor.

Einstein's friend and fellow physicist Abraham Pais called him "the freest man I have known," by which he meant that by the pure act of thinking, Einstein controlled his destiny. His mind was utterly fearless, and by its uses he diminished fear in others. "It stands to the everlasting credit of science," Einstein wrote, "that by acting on the human mind, it has overcome man's insecurity before himself and before nature." And so he became a model of what humans might do if they put their mind to it. ∎

He raised the edifice of the American Century by restoring a nation's promise of plenty and by intervening to save a world enveloped in darkness

Franklin Delano

By **DORIS KEARNS GOODWIN**

From Warm Springs, Ga., where he died, the funeral train moved slowly through the rural South to a service in Washington, then past the now thriving cities of the North, and finally to Hyde Park, N.Y., in the Hudson River Valley, where he was born. Wherever it passed, Americans by the hundreds of thousands stood vigil, those who had loved

him and those who came to witness a momentous passage in the life of the nation. Men stood with their arms around the shoulders of their wives and mothers. They stood in clusters, heads bowed, openly weeping. They clasped their hands in prayer. A father lifted his son so he could see the last car, which carried the flag-draped coffin. "I saw everything," the youngster said. "That's good," the father said. "Now make sure you remember."

He had been President of the United States for 12 of the most tumultuous years in the life of the nation. For many, an America without Roosevelt seemed almost inconceivable. He had guided the nation through democracy's two monumental crises—the Great Depression and World War II. Those who watched the coffin pass were the beneficiaries of his nation's victory. Their children would live to see the

causes for which he stood—prosperity and freedom, economic justice and political democracy—gather strength throughout the century, come to dominate life in America and in much of the world.

It is tempting to view these triumphs as the consequence of irresistible historical forces. But inevitability is merely an illusory label we impose on that which has already happened. It does not tell us what might have happened. For that, we need to view events through the eyes of those who lived them. Looked at that way, we understand that twice in mid-century, capitalism and democracy were in the gravest peril, rescued by the enormous efforts of countless people summoned to struggle by their peerless leader—Franklin Delano Roosevelt.

"Men will thank God on their knees a hundred years from now that Franklin D. Roosevelt was in the White House," the

(1882-1945)

osevelt

> # "Capitalism is dying. Let no one delude himself by hoping for reform from within."
>
> **REINHOLD NIEBUHR, theologian**

With Eleanor at Campobello in 1920; polio would strike the next year

reached nearly 50%. In the countryside, crops that could not be sold at market rotted in the fields. More than half a million homeowners, unable to pay their mortgages, had lost their homes and their farms; thousands of banks had failed, destroying the life savings of millions. The Federal Government had virtually no mechanisms in place to provide relief.

As the Great Depression circled the globe, democracy and capitalism were everywhere in retreat. Propagandists proclaimed that the choice was one of two extremes—fascism or communism. In Germany, economic collapse led to the triumph of the Nazi party and the installation of Adolf Hitler as Chancellor; in Italy, Benito Mussolini assumed dictatorial power with an ideology called Fascism; in the Soviet Union, Joseph Stalin and the communist ideology held sway.

"Capitalism is dying," theologian Reinhold Niebuhr argued. "Let no one delude himself by hoping for reform from within." The American Communist Party believed its moment had come. "If I vote at all," social critic Lewis Mumford said, "it will be for the Communists." "The destruction of the Democratic Party," argued University of Chicago professor Paul Douglas (who would later become a pillar of the same party), "would be one of the best things that could happen in our political life." "The situation is critical," political analyst Walter Lippman warned Roosevelt two months before he took office. "You may have no alternative but to assume dictatorial power."

It was Roosevelt's lasting accomplishment that he found a middle ground between the unbridled laissez-faire of the '20s and the brutal dictatorships of the '30s. His conviction that a democratic government had a responsibility to help Americans in distress—not as a matter of charity but as a matter of social duty—provided a moral compass to guide both his words and his actions. Believing there had never been a time other than the Civil War when democratic institutions had been in such jeopardy, Roosevelt fashioned a New Deal, which fundamentally altered the relationship of the government to its people, rearranged the balance of power between capital and labor and made the industrial system more humane.

Massive public works projects put millions to work building schools, roads, libraries, hospitals; repairing bridges; digging conservation trails; painting murals in public buildings. The Securities and Exchange Commission regulated a stock market that had been run as an insiders' game. Federal funds protected mortgages so that property owners could keep their homes; legislation guaranteed labor's right to organize and established minimum wages and maximum hours. A sweeping Social Security system provided a measure of security and dignity to the elderly.

New York *Times* editorialized at the time of his death. "It was his hand, more than that of any other single man, that built the great coalition of the United Nations. It was his leadership which inspired free men in every part of the world to fight with greater hope and courage. Gone is the fresh and spontaneous interest which this man took, as naturally as he breathed air, in the troubles and the hardships and the disappointments and the hopes of little men and humble people."

Even through the grainy newsreels, we can see what the people at the time saw: the radiant smile, the eyes flashing with good humor, the cigarette holder held at a jaunty angle, the good-natured toss of the head, the buoyant optimism, the serene confidence with which he met economic catastrophe and international crisis.

When Roosevelt assumed the presidency, America was in its third year of depression. No other decline in American history had been so deep, so lasting, so far reaching. Factories that had once produced steel, automobiles, furniture and textiles stood eerily silent. One out of every four Americans was unemployed, and in the cities the number

No factor was more important to Roosevelt's success than his confidence in himself and his unshakable belief in the American people. What is more, he had a remarkable capacity to transmit his cheerful strength to others, to make them believe that if they pulled together, everything would turn out all right. The source of this remarkable confidence can be traced to his earliest days. "All that is in me goes back to the Hudson," Roosevelt liked to say, meaning not simply the peaceful, slow-moving river and the big, comfortable clapboard house but the ambiance of boundless devotion that encompassed him as a child. Growing up in an atmosphere in which affection and respect were plentiful, where the discipline was fair and loving, and the opportunities for self-expression were abundant, he came to trust that the world was basically a friendly and agreeable place. After schooling at Groton, Harvard and Columbia, he practiced law for a short period and then entered what would become his lifelong profession: politics. He won a seat in the New York State senate, became an Assistant Secretary in the Navy Department and ran as the vice-presidential candidate on the Democratic Party's unsuccessful ticket in 1920.

H E WAS 39, AT THE HEIGHT OF HIS POWERS, WHEN HE was stricken with polio and became a paraplegic. He had been an athlete, a man who had loved to swim and sail, to play tennis and golf, to run in the woods and ride horseback in the fields. Determined to overcome his disability, he devoted seven years of his life to grueling physical therapy. In 1928, however, when he accepted the Democratic nomination for Governor of New York, he understood that victory would bring an end to his daily therapy, that he would never walk under his own power again. For the remainder of his life—through four years as Governor of New York and 12 years as President—the mere act of standing up with his heavy metal braces locked in place would be an ordeal. Yet the paralysis that crippled his body expanded his mind and his sensibilities. After what his wife Eleanor called his trial by fire, he seemed less arrogant, less superficial, more focused, more complex, more interesting. "There had been a plowing up of his nature," Labor Secretary Frances Perkins observed. "The man emerged completely warmhearted, with new humility of spirit and a firmer understanding of philosophical concepts." He had always taken great pleasure in people. But now, far more intensely than before, he reached out to know them, to pick up their emotions, to put himself in their shoes. No longer belonging to his old world in the same way, he came to empathize with the poor and the underprivileged, with people to whom fate had dealt a difficult hand.

No other President had so thoroughly occupied the imagination of the American people. Using the new medium of the radio, he spoke directly to them, using simple words and everyday analogies, in a series of "fireside chats," designed not only to shape, educate and move public opinion forward but also to inspire people to act, making them

F.D.R. in an early campaign, opposing Warren Harding

participants in a shared drama. People felt he was talking to them personally, not to millions of others.

After his first address on the banking crisis, in which he explained to families why it was safer to return their money to the banks rather than keep it hidden at home, large deposits began flowing back into the banking system. When he asked everyone to spread a map before them in preparation for a fireside chat on the war in the Pacific, map stores sold more maps in a span of days than they had in an entire year.

Roosevelt purposely limited his fireside talks to an average of two or three a year, in contrast to the modern presidential practice of weekly radio addresses. Timed at dramatic moments, they commanded gigantic audiences, larger than any other program on the radio, including the biggest prizefights and the most popular comedy shows.

The novelist Saul Bellow recalls walking down the street on a hot summer night in Chicago while Roosevelt was speaking. Through lit windows, families could be seen sitting at their kitchen table or gathered in the parlor listening to the radio. Under the elm trees, "drivers had pulled over, parking bumper to bumper, and turned on their radios to hear Roosevelt. They had rolled down the windows and opened the car doors. Everywhere the same voice. You could follow without missing a single word as you strolled by."

The press conference became another critical tool in reaching the hearts and minds of the American people. At his very first conference, he announced he was suspending the wooden practice of requiring written questions submitted in advance. He promised to meet reporters twice a week and by and large kept his promise, holding nearly 1,000 press conferences in the course of his presidency.

F.D.R. chats to homesteader Steve Brown in North Dakota in 1936

Talkative and relaxed, he explained legislation, announced appointments and established friendly contact, calling reporters by their first name, teasing them about their hangovers, exuding warmth. Roosevelt's accessibility to the working journalists helped explain the paradox that though 80% to 85% of the newspaper publishers regularly opposed his policies, his coverage was generally full and fair.

Though the national economy remained in a depressed state until the war broke out, the massive programs of the New Deal had stopped the precipitous slide and provided an economic floor for tens of millions of Americans. "We aren't on relief anymore," one woman noted with pride. "My husband is working for the government." The despair that had hung over the land was lifted, replaced by a bustling sense of movement and activity, a renewed confidence in the future, a revived faith in democracy. "There is a mysterious cycle in human events," Roosevelt said when he accepted his party's nomination for a second term. "To some generations much is given. Of other generations much is expected. This generation has a rendezvous with destiny."

I N 1940 THE U.S. AND THE DEMOCRATIC WAY OF LIFE faced a second crisis even more fearful than the first as Hitler's armies marched through Holland, Belgium, Luxembourg and France, leaving Britain standing alone against the Nazi juggernaut. "Never," Winston Churchill admitted, after the British army was forced to evacuate from Dunkirk, "has a nation been so naked before its foes." At that moment, in all of Britain, there were only 600,000 rifles and 500 cannons, many of them borrowed from museums. With Britain on the verge of defeat, U.S. military leaders were unanimous in urging Roosevelt to stop sending our limited supply of weapons overseas and instead focus on rearming at home. At that time the U.S. Army stood only 18th in the world, trailing not only Germany, France, Britain, Russia, Italy, Japan and China, but also Holland, Spain, and Romania! So strong had been the recoil from war after 1918 that both the government and the private sector had backed away from making weapons, leaving the military with almost no modern planes, tanks or ships.

But Roosevelt was determined to send whatever he could to Britain, even if it meant putting America's short-term security in jeopardy. It was a daring decision. For if Britain were to fall in six months' time, as was predicted, and if Germany turned on the U.S. using our captured weapons, then, one general warned, everyone who was a party to the deal might be found hanging from a lamppost. Undaunted, Roosevelt placed his bet on Britain and its Prime Minister, Churchill. And he was right, for despite the terrifying situation the British found themselves in, with bombs raining down every night on their cities and homes, they picked their way through the rubble every morning to get to work, refusing to be broken, proving Churchill's prediction that if the British and their empire were to last a thousand years, this would be their finest hour.

Eleanor Roosevelt's activities broke the mold for First Ladies

In those desperate days the seeds were planted for a historic friendship between the British Prime Minister and the American President. In the months that followed, Churchill spent weeks at a time at the White House, living in the family quarters on the second floor in a bedroom diagonally across from Roosevelt's. There was something so intimate in their friendship, Churchill's aide Lord Ismay noted. They would stroll in and out of each other's rooms as two schoolboys occupying adjacent dorm rooms might have, staying up until 2 or 3 a.m. talking, drinking brandy and smoking cigars. After each of Churchill's visits, Roosevelt was so exhausted he had to sleep 10 hours a day for three days straight until he recovered. But they took the greatest delight in each other. "It is fun to be in the same decade with you," Roosevelt told Churchill. "If anything happened to that man, I couldn't stand it," Churchill told a U.S. diplomat. "He is the truest friend; he has the farthest vision; he is the greatest man I have ever known."

When Germany invaded Russia in 1941, Roosevelt once again defied prevailing opinion. To the isolationists, the invasion of Russia confirmed the wisdom of keeping America out of the war. America should rejoice, they argued, in watching two hated dictatorships bleed each other to death. Within the government, Roosevelt's military advisers argued that Russia had almost no chance of holding out. Still, Roosevelt insisted on including Russia in the lend-lease agreement. In the first year alone, America sent thousands of trucks, tanks, guns and bombers to Russia, along with enough food to keep Russian soldiers from starving, and enough cotton, blankets, shoes and boots to clothe the entire Russian army. The forbearance of the Russian army, in turn, bought the Allies the precious asset of time—time to mobilize the U.S. economy to produce the vast supply of weapons that was needed to catch up with and eventually surpass the Axis powers.

Roosevelt's critics were certain he would straitjacket the free-enterprise system once America began mobilizing for war. Through his first two terms, Republican businessmen had been driven by an almost primitive hostility to Roosevelt, viewing his support for the welfare state and organized labor as an act of betrayal of his class. Refusing to say his name, they referred to him simply as "that man in the White House." Yet, under Roosevelt's wartime leadership, the government entered into the most productive partnership with private enterprise the country had ever seen,

Even in the early years of the war, when the situation looked bleak, when it seemed impossible that the Allies could overtake the Axis lead, Roosevelt retained an imperturbable calm. To the endless wonder of his aides, he was able to relax and replenish his energies each night to face the struggles of the following day. Every evening he held a cocktail hour where talk of politics or war was outlawed; instead the conversation was deliberately turned to gossip, funny stories or reminiscences. Roosevelt spent untold hours sorting his stamp collection, playing poker with his Cabinet members, watching mystery movies. Only when Eleanor chose the movies would he watch serious films— *The Grapes of Wrath* or a documentary on civil rights.

Allies Roosevelt, Churchill and Stalin meet at Yalta to plan Germany's occupation

bringing top businessmen in to run the production agencies, exempting business from antitrust laws, allowing business to write off the full cost of investments and guaranteeing a substantial profit. The output was staggering. By 1943, American production had not only caught up with Germany's 10-year lead but America was also outproducing all the Axis and the Allied powers combined.

Above all, Roosevelt possessed a magnificent sense of timing. He understood when to invoke the prestige of the presidency and when to hold it in reserve. He picked a first-class military team and gave its members wide latitude to run the war. Yet at critical junctures he forced action, and almost all those actions had a salutary effect on the war. He personally made the hotly debated decision to invade North Africa; he decided to spend $2 billion on an experimental atom bomb; and he demanded the Allies commit themselves to a postwar structure before the war was over.

It was said jokingly in Washington that Roosevelt had a nightly prayer: Dear God, please make Eleanor a little tired. But as Roosevelt himself would be the first to admit, he would never have become the kind of President he was without his tireless wife. She was the agitator dedicated to what should be done; he was the politician concerned with what could be done. It was Eleanor who insisted that the government's wartime partnership with business must not be forged at the expense of labor. It was Eleanor who insisted that America could not fight racism abroad while tolerating it at home. It was Eleanor who championed the movement of women into the work force. Many joined her in these efforts—civil rights leaders, labor leaders, liberal spokesmen. But her passionate voice in the highest councils of decision was always influential and often decisive.

To be sure, Franklin Roosevelt was far from perfect. Critics lamented his deviousness, his lack of candor, his tendency to ingratitude. His character flaws were widely

" He is the truest friend; he has the farthest vision; he is the greatest man I have ever known. "

WINSTON CHURCHILL, on Roosevelt

discussed: his stubbornness, his vanity, his occasional vindictiveness, his habit of yessing callers just to be amiable. At times, his confidence merged into arrogance, diminishing his political instincts and leading to an ill-defined court-packing scheme and an unsuccessful attempt to purge his opponents in the 1938 by-elections. One must also concede the failures of vision that led to the forcible relocation of Japanese Americans, which deprived tens of thousands of men, women and children of Japanese descent of their fundamental civil liberties, and the devastating failure to bring more Jewish refugees into America, beyond Hitler's grasp.

But in the end, Roosevelt's great strengths far outweighed his weaknesses. As the tide of war began to turn decisively, in the year before his death, Roosevelt began to put in place the elements of his vision for the world to come. It was to be a world in which all peoples were entitled to govern themselves. With this aim, he foresaw the end of the colonial imperialism that had dominated much of the globe. Through the U.N., which he was instrumental in establishing, we would, he hoped, finally have an international structure for peace-keeping. His call for recognition of four universal freedoms so firmly charted the still unfinished agenda for humanity that a recent British publication, assessing the century, noted that Roosevelt's Four Freedoms—from fear and from want, and of belief and expression—are possessed by more people, more securely, than ever before. Today, more than a half-century after his death, Roosevelt's vision, still unfulfilled, still endangered, remains the guardian spirit for the noblest and most humane impulses of mankind.

When he died, even his most partisan adversaries felt compelled to acknowledge the immensity of the man they had opposed. Senator Robert Taft, known as Mr. Republican, considered Roosevelt's death a tragedy. As Eleanor traveled the land in the months after her husband's demise, she was overwhelmed by the emotion of all the people who came up to her—porters at the station, taxi drivers, doormen, elevator operators, riders in the subway—and told her how much better their lives were because of his leadership.

Blacks talked of the pride they felt in the work they had accomplished at home, the courage they had shown in their battalions abroad—a pride that would soon fuel the civil rights movement. Women talked of the camaraderie, the feelings of accomplishment they had experienced in the shipyards and the factories. And even though the factories were firing the women that summer and closing down the day-care centers that would not reopen for a generation, Eleanor could see that there had been a change of consciousness that would mean no turning back. She talked to G.I.s who were going to college on Roosevelt's G.I. Bill of Rights, the remarkable piece of legislation that opened the door to the upward mobility of an entire generation. A social revolution had taken place; a new economic order had come into being; a vast middle class had been born.

An image formed in Eleanor's mind, that during the course of her husband's presidency a giant transference of energy had taken place between him and the people. In the early days, the country was fragile, weak and isolationist, while her husband was full of energy, vital and productive. But gradually, as the President animated his countrymen with his strength and confidence, the people grew stronger and stronger, while he grew weaker and weaker, until in the end he was so weakened he died, but the country emerged more powerful, more productive and more socially just than it had ever been before.

Eleanor's image was, to be sure, a romanticized view of her husband's presidency, but it suggests the ultimate mystery of Roosevelt's leadership—his ability to use his moral authority, the degree of confidence he inspired, to strengthen the people and bind them together in a just cause.

It may well be true that crisis and war provide a unity of purpose and an opportunity for leadership that are rarely present in more tranquil times. But as the history of other countries illustrates, war and domestic upheaval are no guarantee of positive social change. That depends on the time, the nation and the exercise of leadership. In providing the indispensable leadership that preserved and strengthened democracy, Franklin Roosevelt emerges as the greatest political leader of the age. ■

Doris Kearns Goodwin is a Pulitzer-prizewinning author, historian and political analyst.

At Hyde Park, F.D.R. chats with the caretaker's granddaughter

The President
on the deck of
the U.S.S.
Houston in 1939

Captain
Courageous

The U.S. President weighs F.D.R.'s legacy and finds timeless fortitude, persistence and respect for the common man

By BILL CLINTON

W HEN OUR CHILDREN'S CHILDREN READ THE story of the 20th century, they will see that above all, it is the story of freedom's triumph: the victory of democracy over fascism and totalitarianism; of free enterprise over command economies; of tolerance over bigotry. And they will see that the embodiment of that triumph, the driving force behind it, was Franklin Delano Roosevelt.

In the century's struggle for freedom, Roosevelt won two decisive victories: first over economic depression and then over fascism. Though he was surrounded by turmoil, he envisioned a world of lasting peace, and he devoted his life to building a new era of progress. Roosevelt's leadership steered not only America but also the world through the roughest seas of the century. And he did it with a combination of skilled statesmanship, innovative spirit and, as Oliver Wendell Holmes Jr. put it, "a first-class temperament."

Even though Franklin Roosevelt was the architect of grand designs, he touched tens of millions of Americans in a very personal way. When I first worked on political campaigns in the 1960s, I couldn't help noticing the pictures of F.D.R. that graced the walls and mantels of so many of the homes I visited. To ordinary Americans, Roosevelt was more than a great President: he was part of the family.

My own grandfather felt the same way. He came from a little town of about 50 people, had only a fourth-grade education and owned a small store. Still, he believed this President was a friend, a man who cared about him and his family's future. My grandfather was right about that. So were the millions of Americans who met President Roosevelt only through his radio fireside chats. Roosevelt earned his place in the homes and hearts of a whole generation.

As a state legislator, Governor and President, Roosevelt pioneered the politics of inclusion. He built a broad, lasting, national coalition uniting different regions, different classes and different races. He identified with the aspirations of immigrants, farmers and factory workers—"the forgotten Americans," as he called them. He considered them citizens of America just as fully as he was.

ROOSEVELT KNEW IN THE MARROW OF HIS BONES, from his own struggle with polio and his innate grasp of the American temper, that restoring optimism was the beginning of progress. "The only thing we have to fear is fear itself" was both the way he led his life and the way he led our nation. No matter what the challenge, he believed that the facts were only one part of reality; the other part was how you react to them and change them for the better. In the depths of the Great Depression, the gravest economic threat the country ever faced, he lifted the nation to its feet and into action.

From his vision emerged the great American middle class that has been the engine of more than five decades of progress and prosperity. From his new ideas flowed the seemingly endless array of programs and agencies of the New Deal: bank reform, rural electrification, the G.I. Bill. And, of course, his most enduring domestic creation, Social Security, a bond between generations that every President since has honored. Roosevelt proved that for markets to flourish, government must be devoted to opportunity for all. He understood that the initiative of individuals and the responsibilities of community must be woven together.

To defeat the merciless aggression of fascism, President Roosevelt created an international alliance to defend freedom, and he committed the U.S. to lead it. He proved that our liberty is linked to the destiny of the world, that our security requires us to support democracy beyond our shores, that human rights must be America's cause. In the 20th century's greatest crisis, Roosevelt decisively, irrevocably committed our country to freedom's fight.

Early in World War II, he defined the Four Freedoms that he said must be realized everywhere in the world: freedom of speech, freedom of worship, freedom from want, freedom from fear. These were, in his own words, "essential human freedoms." His expression of American ideals helped make them the world's ideals. Because of that commitment and its embrace by every American President since, today we can say, for the first time in history, a majority of the world's people live under governments of their own choosing.

Roosevelt's leadership in war and his commitment to peace established the institutions of collective security that have prevented another world conflagration. The whole system of international cooperation stems from his commitment. It was President Roosevelt, after all, who conceived and named the United Nations, and he was one of the visionaries behind international financial cooperation.

Much of my own political philosophy and approach to governance is rooted in Roosevelt's principles of progress. That's why one of the first things I did after I became President was make a pilgrimage to Hyde Park. And that's why when England's Prime Minister Tony Blair came to visit, I took him on a tour of the F.D.R. Memorial. Rather than cling to old abstractions or be driven by the iron laws of ideology, Roosevelt crafted innovative, practical solutions to the challenges he faced. He called his pragmatic method "bold, persistent experimentation." If one thing doesn't work, he explained, "try another; but above all, try something."

Winston Churchill remarked that Franklin Roosevelt's life was one of the commanding events in human history. The triumph of freedom in the face of depression and totalitarianism was not foretold or inevitable. It required political courage and leadership. We now know what Roosevelt and his generation made of their "rendezvous with destiny." Their legacy is our world of freedom. If the example of Franklin Roosevelt and the American Century has taught us anything, it is that either we will work together as One America to shape events or we will be shaped by them. We cannot isolate ourselves from the world; we cannot lead in fits and starts. Now, to this generation entering the new millennium, as Roosevelt said, "much has been given" and "much is expected." ■

President Bill Clinton, history buff (and Democrat), cast his vote for Franklin Roosevelt as TIME'*s Person of the Century.*

Naval CPO Graham Jackson weeps as he plays a dirge after Roosevelt's death

In an age of imperial might, he proved that the powerless had power and that force of arms would not forever prevail against force of spirit

(1869-1948) **Mohandas**

By JOHANNA McGEARY

The Mahatma, the Great Soul, endures in the best part of our minds, where our ideals are kept: the embodiment of human rights and the creed of nonviolence. Mohandas Karamchand Gandhi is something else, an eccentric of complex, contradictory and exhausting character most of us hardly know. It is fashionable at this fin de siècle to use the man to tear down the hero, to expose human pathologies at the expense of larger-than-life achievements. No myth raking can rob Gandhi of his moral force or diminish the remarkable importance of this scrawny little man. For the 20th century—and surely for the ones to follow—it is the towering example of the Mahatma that matters.

Consciously or not, oppressed peoples or groups with a cause have practiced what Gandhi preached. Sixties kids like me were his disciples when we went south in the Freedom Summer to sit in for civil rights and when we paraded through the streets of America to stop the war in Vietnam. Our passionate commitment, nonviolent activism and willingness to accept punishment for civil disobedience were lessons he taught. Martin Luther King Jr. learned them; so did Nelson Mandela, Lech Walesa, Aung San Suu Kyi, the unknown man who defied the Chinese tanks in 1989 and the environmental marchers who shut down Seattle late in 1999.

It may be that this most Indian of leaders, revered as Bapuji, or Father of the Nation, means more now to the world at large. Foreigners don't have to wrestle with the confusion Indians feel today as they judge whether their nation has kept faith with his vision. For the rest of us, his image offers something much simpler—a shining set of ideals to emulate. Individual freedom. Political liberty. Social justice. Nonviolent protest. Passive resistance. Religious tolerance. His labors and his spirit awakened the 20th century to ideas

ndhi

O'BRIEN

"Men like him redeem us from a sense of commonplace and futility."

JAN SMUTS, Gandhi's political adversary in South Africa

At his Johannesburg law office in British-ruled South Africa

larity in his daily regimen that he safety-pinned a watch to his homespun dhoti, synchronized with the clock at his ashram. He scheduled his bowel movements for 20 minutes, morning and afternoon. "The bathroom is a temple," he declared, and anyone was welcome to chat with him there. He had a cleansing enema every night.

Gandhi bathed in water but used ashes instead of soap and had himself shaved with a dull straight razor; new blades were too expensive. He was always sweeping up excrement that others left around. Cleanliness, he believed, was godliness. But his passion for sanitation was not just finicky hygiene. He wanted to teach Indian villagers that human and animal filth caused most of the disease in the land.

Every afternoon, Gandhi did an hour or two of spinning on his little handwheel, sometimes 400 yards at a sitting. "I am spinning the destiny of India," he would say. He hoped his example would convince Indians that homespun could free them from dependence on foreign products. But the real point of the spinning was to teach appreciation for manual labor, restore self-respect lost to colonial subjugation and cultivate inner strength.

The man was not unaware of his legend in the making—or the 90-plus volumes that would eventually be needed to preserve his words. Everything Gandhi ever said and did was recorded by legions of secretaries. Then he insisted on going over their notes and choosing the version he liked best. "I want only one gospel in my life," he said.

A strange amalgam of beliefs formed the complicated core of Gandhism. History will merely smile at his railing against Western ways, industrialism and material pleasures. He never stopped calling for a nation that would turn its back on technology to prosper through village self-sufficiency, but not even the Mahatma could hold back progress. Yet many today share his uneasiness with the way mechanization and materialism sicken the human spirit.

MORE CENTRAL AND EVEN MORE CONTROVERSIAL was Gandhi's cult of celibacy. At 13, he dutifully married and came quickly to lust for his wife Kasturba. At 16 he left his dying father's side to make love to her. His father died that night, and Gandhi could never forgive himself the "double shame." He neglected and even humiliated Kasturba most of his life and only after her death realized she was "the warp and woof of my life." At 36, convinced that sex was the basis of all impulses that must be mastered if man was to reach Truth, he renounced it. An aspirant to a godly life must observe the Hindu practice of Brahmacharya, or celibacy, as a means of self-control and a way to devote all energy to public service. Gandhi spent years testing his self-discipline by sleeping beside young women. He evidently cared little about any psychological damage to them.

Gandhi sought God, not orthodoxy. His daily prayers mixed traditional Hindu venerations with Buddhist chants, readings from the Koran, Zoroastrian verses and the Christian hymn *Lead, Kindly Light*. That eclecticism reflected his

that will continue to serve as a moral beacon for all epochs.

Half a century after his death, most of us know little of Gandhi's real history or how the Mahatma in our minds came to be. Hundreds of biographies uncritically canonize him. Winston Churchill scorned him as a half-naked fakir stirring up sedition. His generation knew him as a radical political agitator; ours shrugs off a holy man with romantic notions of a pure, pre-industrial life. There is no either-or. The saint and the politician inhabited the same slender frame, each nourishing the other. His struggle for a nation's rights fused with his struggle for individual salvation.

The flesh-and-blood Gandhi was a most unlikely saint. Just conjure up his portrait: a skinny, bent figure, nut brown and naked except for a white loincloth, cheap spectacles perched on his nose, frail hand grasping a tall bamboo staff. This was one of the century's great revolutionaries? Yes, and this strange figure swayed millions with his hypnotic spell. His garb was the perfect uniform for the kind of revolutionary he was, wielding weapons of prayer and nonviolence more powerful than guns.

Saints are hard to live with, and this one's personal habits were decidedly odd. Mondays were "days of silence," when he refused to speak. A devoted vegetarian, he indulged in faddish dietetic experiments that sometimes came near to killing him. He eschewed all spices as a discipline of the senses. He napped every day with a mud poultice on his abdomen and brow. He was so insistent on absolute regu-

great tolerance for all religions, one of his holiest—and least respected—precepts. "Truth," he preached, "is God," but he could never persuade India's warring religious sects to agree. His spiritual mentors were just as broad—Jesus, Buddha, Socrates, his mother, whose "saintliness" and devout asceticism infused his soul. The family's brand of Hinduism schooled him in the sacredness of all God's creatures.

While studying in England to be a lawyer, he first read the Bible and the Bhagavad Gita, the Hindu religious poem that became his "spiritual dictionary." For Gandhi, the epic was a clarion call to the soul to undertake the battle of righteousness. It taught him to renounce personal desires not by withdrawal from the world but by devotion to the service of his fellow man. In the Christian New Testament he felt the stirrings of passive resistance in the words of the Sermon on the Mount.

Those credos came together in the two principles that ruled his public life: what he called Satyagraha, the force of truth and love; and the ancient Hindu ideal of ahimsa, or nonviolence to all living things. He first put those principles to political work in South Africa, where he had gone to practice law and tasted raw discrimination. Traveling to Johannesburg in a first-class train compartment, he was ordered to move to the "colored" cars in the rear. When he refused, he was hauled off the train and left to spend a freezing night in the station. The next day he was humiliated and cuffed by the white driver of a stagecoach. The experience steeled his resolve to fight for social justice.

In 1906, confronting a government move to fingerprint all Indians, Gandhi countered with a new idea—"passive resistance," securing political rights through personal suffering and the power of truth and love. "Indians," he wrote, "will stagger humanity without shedding a drop of blood." He failed to provoke legal changes, and Indians gained little more than a newfound self-respect. But even his principal adversary, Afrikaner leader Jan Smuts, said, "Men like

Gandhi's single most successful protest, the salt march of 1930, brilliantly dramatized the unfairness of the British colonial system

> **Everybody is eager to garland my photos. But nobody wants to follow my advice.**
>
> MOHANDAS GANDHI, after India's independence was won

He sought to free Indians not only from the British, but also from modern technologies, which he believed demeaned their spirits

him redeem us from a sense of commonplace and futility."

South Africa was dress rehearsal for Gandhi's great cause, independence for India. From the day he arrived back home at 45, he dedicated himself to "Hind swaraj," Indian self-rule. More than independence, it meant a utopian blend of national liberty and social justice. Freedom also entailed individual emancipation, the search for nobility of soul through self-discipline and denial. Most ordinary Indians, though, simply sought an end to colonial rule. While his peace-and-love homilies may not have swayed them, they followed him because he made the British tremble.

Gandhi quickly became a commanding figure who brooked no challenge to his ultimate leadership. The force of his convictions transformed the Indian National Congress from upper-class movement to mass crusade. He made his little spinning wheel a physical bond between élite and illiterate when both donned the khadi cloth.

In the next 33 years, he led three major crusades to undermine the power and moral defenses of the British Raj. In 1919-22 he mustered widespread nonviolent strikes, then a campaign of peaceful noncooperation, urging Indians to boycott anything British—schools, courts, goods, even the English language. He believed mass noncooperation would achieve independence within a year. Instead, it degenerated into bloody rioting, and British soldiers turned their guns on a crowd in Amritsar, massacring 400. Still, villagers mobbed him wherever he went, calling him Mahatma. By 1922, 30,000 followers had been jailed, and Gandhi ordered civil disobedience. The British slowed the momentum by jailing him for 22 months.

Gandhi was never a man to give up. On March 12, 1930, he launched a brilliant stroke, national defiance of the law forbidding Indians to make their own salt. With 78 followers, he set out for the coast to make salt until the law was

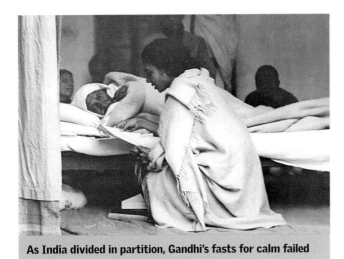

As India divided in partition, Gandhi's fasts for calm failed

repealed. By the time he reached the sea, people all across the land had joined in. Civil disobedience spread until Gandhi was arrested again. Soon more than 60,000 Indians filled the jails, and Britain was shamed by the gentle power of the old man and his unresisting supporters. Though Gandhi had been elected to no office and represented no government, the Viceroy soon began negotiating with him.

World War II caught him by surprise. The unremitting pacifist did not grasp the evil of Hitler because he thought no man beyond redemption. He deeply offended Jews when he counseled them to follow the path of nonviolence. Gandhi did not want Britain's defeat, but recognized a political opportunity. In late 1940 he agreed to a modest campaign of individual civil disobedience.

But other politicians pressed hard for nonviolent mass struggle against a weakened Raj. In 1942 Gandhi reluctantly endorsed the Quit India plan, calling on London for Indian independence. He and the Congress leaders were arrested and jailed. Huge demonstrations soon flared into rioting and revolt. The Raj struck back hard; nearly 1,000 Indians were killed before the uprising flamed out. Gandhi was finally freed on May 5, 1944. He had spent 2,338 days of his 74 years imprisoned.

By war's end, Britain was ready to let India go. But the moment of Gandhi's greatest triumph, on Aug. 15, 1947, was also the hour of his defeat. India gained freedom but lost unity when Britain granted independence on the same day it created the new Muslim state of Pakistan. Partition dishonored Gandhi's sect-blind creed. "There is no message at all," he said that day.

At 77, he despaired that "my life's work seems to be over." Resentment of Britain had been replaced by religious hatred. The killing before partition made it inevitable, and the slaughter afterward trampled on his appeals for tolerance and trust. All the village pilgrimages he made in 1946 and 1947 could not stop Muslims and Hindus from murdering one another. All the famous fasts he undertook could not persuade them to live in harmony. He blamed himself when Indians rejected nonviolence.

Assassination made him a martyr. The Hindu fanatic who fired three bullets into Gandhi at point-blank range on Jan. 30, 1948, blamed him for letting Muslims steal part of the Hindu nation, for not hating Muslims. Free at last thanks to his efforts, India found him irrelevant.

Today interest in the flesh-and-blood Mohandas Karamchand has faded away. We revere the Mahatma while ignoring half of what he taught. Yet Gandhi is that rare great man held in universal esteem, a figure lifted from daily life to moral icon. He stamped his ideas on history, igniting three of the century's great revolutions—against colonialism, racism, violence. His concept of nonviolent resistance liberated one nation and sped the end of colonial empires around the world. His marches and fasts fired the imagination of oppressed people everywhere. Like the millions of Indians who pressed around his funeral cortege seeking darshan—contact with his sanctity—millions more have sought freedom and justice under the Mahatma's guiding light. He shines as a conscience for the world. The saint and the politician go hand in hand, proclaiming the power of love, peace and freedom. ∎

After cremation, his ashes were strewn where the Jumna and Ganges rivers meet

The Sacred Warrior

The liberator of South Africa looks at the seminal work of the liberator of India

By NELSON MANDELA

INDIA IS GANDHI'S COUNTRY OF BIRTH; SOUTH AFRICA his country of adoption. He was both an Indian and a South African citizen. Both countries contributed to his intellectual and moral genius, and he shaped the liberatory movements in both colonial theaters. He is the archetypal anticolonial revolutionary. His strategy of noncooperation, his assertion that we can be dominated only if we cooperate with our dominators, and his nonviolent resistance inspired anticolonial and antiracist movements internationally in our century.

Both Gandhi and I suffered colonial oppression, and both of us mobilized our respective peoples against governments that violated our freedoms. The Gandhian influence dominated freedom struggles on the African continent right up to the 1960s because of the power it generated and the unity it forged among the apparently powerless. Nonviolence was the official stance of all major African coalitions, and my party, the African National Congress, remained implacably opposed to violence for most of its existence.

Gandhi remained committed to nonviolence; I followed the Gandhian strategy for as long as I could, but there came a point in our struggle when the brute force of the oppressor could no longer be countered through passive resistance alone. We founded Unkhonto we Sizwe and added a military dimension to our struggle. Even then, we chose sabotage because it did not involve the loss of life, and it offered the best hope for future race relations. Militant action became part of the African agenda in 1962, when I stated, "Force is the only language the imperialists can hear, and no country became free without some sort of violence."

Gandhi himself never ruled out violence absolutely and unreservedly. He conceded the necessity of arms in certain situations. He said, "Where choice is set between cowardice and violence, I would advise violence ... I prefer to use arms in defense of honor rather than remain the vile witness of dishonor ..." Violence and nonviolence are not mutually exclusive; it is the predominance of the one or the other that labels a struggle.

Gandhi arrived in South Africa in 1893 at the age of 23. Within a week he collided head on with racism. His immediate response was to flee the country that so degraded people of color, but then his inner resilience overpowered him with a sense of mission, and he stayed to redeem the dignity of the racially exploited, to pave the way for the liberation of the colonized the world over and to develop a blueprint for a new social order. He left 21 years later, a near Mahatma (great soul). There is no doubt in my mind that by the time he was violently removed from our world, he had transited into that state.

He was no ordinary leader. There are those who believe he was divinely inspired, and it is difficult not to believe with them. He dared to exhort nonviolence in a time when the violence of Hiroshima had exploded on us; he exhorted morality when science, technology and the capitalist order had made it redundant; he replaced self-interest with group interest without minimizing the importance of self. In fact, the interdependence of the social and the personal is at the heart of his philosophy, which seeks the simultaneous and interactive development of the moral person and the moral society.

His philosophy of Satyagraha is both a personal and a social struggle to realize the Truth, which he identifies as God, the Absolute Morality. He seeks this Truth, not in isolation, self-centeredly, but with the people. He said, "I want to find God, and because I want to find God, I have to find God along with other people. I don't believe I can find God alone. If I did, I would be running to the Himalayas to find God in some cave there." Thus Gandhi sacercises his revolution, balancing the religious and the secular.

> # I prefer to use arms in defense of honor rather than remain the vile witness of dishonor.

MOHANDAS GANDHI

His awakening came on the hilly terrain of the so-called Bambata Rebellion, where as a passionate British patriot, he led his Indian stretcher-bearers to serve the Empire. But British brutality against the Zulus roused his soul against violence as nothing had done before. He determined, on that battlefield, to wrest himself of all material attachments and devote himself completely and totally to eliminating violence and serving humanity. The sight of wounded and whipped Zulus, mercilessly abandoned by their British persecutors, so appalled him that he turned full circle from his

Bringing power to the people: Gandhi, left, and Mandela

admiration for all things British to celebrating the indigenous and ethnic. He resuscitated the culture of the colonized; he revived Indian handicrafts and made these into an economic weapon against the colonizer in his call for *swadeshi*—the use of one's own and the boycott of the oppressor's products, which deprive the people of their skills and their capital.

A GREAT MEASURE OF WORLD POVERTY TODAY AND African poverty in particular is due to the continuing dependence on foreign markets for manufactured goods, which undermines domestic production and dams up domestic skills, apart from piling up unmanageable foreign debts. Gandhi's insistence on self-sufficiency is a basic economic principle that, if followed today, could contribute significantly to alleviating Third World poverty and stimulating development.

Gandhi predated Frantz Fanon and black-consciousness movements in South Africa and the U.S. by more than a half-century and inspired the resurgence of the indigenous intellect, spirit and industry. He rejects the Adam Smith notion of human nature as motivated by self-interest and brute needs and returns us to our spiritual dimension with its impulses for nonviolence, justice and equality. He exposes the fallacy of the claim that everyone can be rich if they

work hard. He points to the millions who work themselves to the bone and still remain hungry. He preaches the gospel of leveling down, of emulating the *kisan* (peasant), not the *zamindar* (landlord), for "all can be *kisans*, but only a few *zamindars*." He stepped down from his comfortable life to join the masses on their level to seek equality with them. "I can't hope to bring about economic equality … I have to reduce myself to the level of the poorest of the poor."

From his understanding of wealth and poverty came his understanding of labor and capital, which led him to the solution of trusteeship based on the belief that there is no private ownership of capital; it is given in trust for redistribution and equalization. Similarly, while recognizing differential aptitudes and talents, he holds that these are gifts from God to be used for the collective good. He seeks an alternative to capitalism and communism, and finds this in *sarvodaya* based on nonviolence (*ahimsa*).

He rejects Darwin's survival of the fittest, Adam Smith's laissez-faire and Karl Marx's thesis of a natural antagonism between capital and labor, and focuses on the interdependence between the two. He believes in the human capacity to change and wages Satyagraha against the oppressor, not to destroy him but to transform him, that he cease his oppression and join the oppressed in the pursuit of Truth. We in South Africa brought about our new democracy relatively peacefully on the foundations of such thinking, whether we were directly influenced by Gandhi or not.

Gandhi remains today the only complete critique of advanced industrial society. Others have criticized its totalitarianism but not its productive apparatus. He is not against science and technology, but he places priority on the right to work and opposes mechanization to the extent that it usurps this right. Large-scale machinery, he holds, concentrates wealth in the hands of one man who tyrannizes the rest. He favors the small machine; he seeks to keep the individual in control of his tools, to maintain an interdependent love relation between the two, as a cricketer with his bat or Krishna with his flute. Above all, he seeks to liberate the individual from his alienation to the machine and restore morality to the productive process. As we find ourselves in jobless economies, societies in which small minorities consume while the masses starve, we find ourselves forced to rethink the rationale of our current globalization and to ponder the Gandhian alternative.

At a time when Freud was liberating sex, Gandhi was reining it in; when Marx was pitting worker against capitalist, Gandhi was reconciling them; when the dominant European thought had dropped God and soul out of the social reckoning, he was centralizing society in God and soul; at a time when the colonized had ceased to think and control, he dared to think and control; and when the ideologies of the colonized had virtually disappeared, he revived and empowered them with a potency that liberated and redeemed. ■

Nelson Mandela served as the first democratically elected President of South Africa from 1994 to 1999.

The Children of Gandhi

His innovative strategy of nonviolence spawned generations of spiritual heirs around the world

The U.S.: Cesar Chavez

The United Farm Workers leader, right, organized pickets, boycotts and, inspired by the Mahatma, hunger strikes. Agreeing with Gandhi, Chavez said, "Fasting is the last resort in place of the sword."

South Africa: Desmond Tutu

The Anglican archbishop, below, fought apartheid while Mandela was in prison. "All violence is evil," he warned, "but a time may come when you have to decide between two evils—oppression or a violent overthrow of the oppressive regime." "When the honor of God is at stake," he said, "we will disobey iniquitous and unjust laws."

The U.S.: Larry Kramer

The notoriously cantankerous playwright, above, inspired ACT-UP's famously confrontational protests for an AIDS cure in the late '80s. As a result, gay and lesbian civil rights remain at the center of American public debate.

Tibet: The Dalai Lama

At the site of Gandhi's cremation, he said, "To me, he was ... the consummate politician, a man who put his belief in altruism above any personal considerations. I was convinced too that his devotion to the cause of nonviolence was the only way to conduct politics."

Myanmar: Aung San Suu Kyi

Under house arrest, the opposition leader, below, continues to espouse nonviolence, despite the junta's tactics. Fighting, she says, "will perpetuate the tradition that he who is best at wielding arms, wields power."

The U.S.: Martin Luther King Jr.

To desegregate Nashville's lunch counters in 1958, King, right, brought in James Lawson, a student of Gandhi's, to train protesters in nonviolence. After his arrest and detention in 1963, his "Letter from a Birmingham Jail" stirred the nation with his account of his nonviolent pursuit of social justice. "Injustice anywhere is a threat to justice everywhere," he wrote—a deeply Gandhian view.

The Necessary Evil?

Why all Adolf Hitler's destructiveness is not enough to make him the Person of the Century

By NANCY GIBBS

HOW CAN YOU NOT PICK HITLER, DEMAND THE players around the table who take seriously the rules of TIME's parlor game: Who had the greatest impact on this century, for better or worse? It is too easy just to say that he lost, when in doing so he still changed everything. It was he who opened the veins of the Bloody Century, an epoch that has seen mayhem on a scale unimagined for centuries. "As a result of Hitler," argued Elie Wiesel in TIME last year, "man is defined by what makes him inhuman." And while the Reich lasted 12 years rather than 1,000, its spores still survive and multiply. "The essence of Hitlerism—racism, ethnic hatred, extreme nationalism, state-organized murder—is still alive, still causing millions of deaths," wrote U.N. Ambassador Richard Holbrooke when he reluctantly nominated Hitler as the century's dominant person. "Freedom is the century's most powerful idea, but the struggle is far from over."

You could ask this of any year, any century: Which has the greater impact, good or evil, the heroes or the villains, Roosevelt and Churchill or Hitler and Stalin? To what extent do they depend on each other, when threats produce resolve, when terror engenders courage, when an ultimate challenge to principle has the effect of making principles stronger, forging them by fire? Thoughtful people who argue for Hitler as the Person of the Century do not want to honor him; they want to autopsy him, understand what made him strong and what finally killed him, and search, perhaps, for a vaccine for the virus that reappears still in ethnic enclaves, on websites, in the wilderness camps of skinhead anarchists and in the halls of Columbine High School, where two boys celebrated Hitler's birthday in 1999 with a memorial massacre of children.

If impact were measured only in number of lives lost, one argument goes, Hitler would fall behind his fellow despots, Stalin and Mao. There are those who insist that

Hitler is not the century's dominant figure because he was simply the latest in a long line of murderous figures, stretching back to before Genghis Khan. The only difference was technology: Hitler went about his cynical carnage with all the brisk efficiency that modern industry had perfected.

And then there is the problem of impact. Which matters more, a life lost or a life changed forever? "How many divisions does the Pope have?" Stalin asked. Yet an idea that alters lives can have more power than an army that takes them: thus Gutenberg presides over the 15th century, Jefferson over the 18th. Making body counts the ultimate measure of influence precludes the possibility of heroic sacrifice, a single death that inspires countless others, a young man in front of a column of tanks near Tiananmen Square. "Five hundred years from now, it won't be Hitler we remember," says theologian Martin Marty. "Hitler may have set the century's agenda; he was a sort of vortex of negative energy that sucked everything else in. But I think God takes fallible human beings like Roosevelt or Churchill and carves them for his purposes. In five centuries, we'll look back and say the story of the century was not Hitler or Stalin; it was the survival of the human spirit in the face of genocide."

If all Hitler had done was kill people in vast numbers more efficiently than anyone else ever did, the debate over

Adolf Hitler was the century's master propagandist. Here he presides over a Nazi rally in Bückeburg in 1934

his lasting importance might end there. But Hitler's impact went beyond his willingness to kill without mercy. He did something civilization had not seen before. Genghis Khan operated in the context of the nomadic steppe, where pillaging villages was the norm. Hitler came out of the most civilized society on earth, the land of Beethoven and Goethe. He set out to kill people not for what they did but for who they were. Even Mao and Stalin killed their "class enemies," while Hitler killed a million Jewish babies just for existing.

It is this distinction that pulls us right into the heart of the question. And that is our long, modern conversation over the nature of evil. The debate goes back to Socrates, who argued that anyone who was acquainted with good could not intentionally choose evil instead. Enlightenment thinkers went further, pushing concepts of good and evil

into the realm of superstition. But Hitler changed that. It was he, perhaps more than any other figure, who demanded a whole rethinking about good, evil, God and man.

"Before Hitler, we thought we had sounded the depths of human nature," argues Ron Rosenbaum, author of *Explaining Hitler*. "He showed how much lower we could go, and that's what was so horrifying. It gets us wondering not just at the depths he showed us but whether there is worse to come." The power of Hitler was to confound the modernist notion that judgments about good and evil were little more than matters of taste, reflections of social class and power and status. Although some modern scholars drive past the notion of evil and instead explain Hitler's conduct as a reflection of his childhood and self-esteem issues, for most survivors of the 20th century he confirms our instinctive

" Freedom is the century's most powerful idea, but the struggle is far from over. "

RICHARD HOLBROOKE, U.S. Ambassador to the United Nations

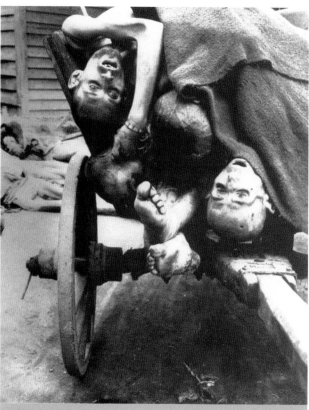

Some argue it took Hitler's sins to redefine democratic ideals

sense that evil does exist. It moves among us; it leads us astray and deploys powerful, subtle weapons against even the sturdiest souls. Hitler had millions of collaborators.

There is a more nuanced, even insidious, argument for Hitler's pre-eminence: that good and evil are dependent on one another. It is a basic tenet to many religions that evil, while mysterious, may clear the way for good, that the soul is perfected only in battle, that pain and ecstasy are somehow twins, that only a soul—or a century—that has truly suffered can truly realize joy. We sense this instinctively—the pleasure we feel when a tooth stops hurting reminds us that we live our life in contexts and contrasts, and so perhaps you can argue that only by witnessing, and confronting, great evil were the forces of light able to burn most bright.

There are theologians and historians who have made this point. Most explicit are those who have called Hitler God's punishment of European Jews for their secularization, then gone on to argue that it was mainly because of him and his Holocaust that the biblical prophecy was fulfilled and the state of Israel born—only Western guilt on so massive a scale could have cleared the way to the Promised Land.

There is a political version of this equation: that at the turn of the century, the West was ruled by thin-blooded despots, with the exception of the more entrenched democracies of England and the U.S. Hitler did not believe the Western democracies capable of defending the principles they espoused—and as they wavered and appeased and betrayed as he expanded, Hitler appeared to be right.

It was Churchill first, and then Roosevelt, who reawakened the West to its core values: freedom, civility, common decency in the face of evil, destructive forces of hate. The challenge presented by Hitler forced Churchill and Roosevelt and the lovers of freedom to battle the great diseases of the century: nihilism and defeatism. Churchill's apostles argue for him as the century's titan on these grounds. In the dark days of 1940, his optimism about victory and his conviction that there were truths worth defending to the death were as important as his identifying the threat and standing up to it. Forty years later, when Ronald Reagan approached the cold war as a battle to be not only fought but also won, he was following a Churchillian strategy.

SO DID IT REQUIRE A HITLER, A MORTAL THREAT, TO move the Allied democracies from complacent enclaves to the global powerhouses that by century's end would embrace most of the world's people? Here is a place to draw the line. "It may be true that we've got great medical breakthroughs, radar, sonar because of war," says theologian Marty, "but I don't like to make a theology out of that; it's an accidental product." Rosenbaum agrees that to focus on the benefits is to risk trivializing the tragedy itself. "There are a lot of people who want to say God was teaching us a lesson—evil is there so that we can learn by struggling against it. I find it kind of barbaric to envision a God who needs to slaughter a million babies in order to perhaps improve our character. I'm irritated by people who try to find some happy-ever-after improving lesson from this."

However much stronger the Western democracies were after the war, as they went on to discredit not only fascism but communism as well, that strength still came at a terrible cost. "How much happier a world it would be if one did not have to mount crusades against racism, segregation, a Holocaust, the extermination of 'inferior peoples,'" notes presidential historian Robert Dallek. "We don't need evil. We'd do fine without Hitler, Stalin, Pol Pot. Think of the amount of money and energy used in World War II—if only they could have been used in constructive ways. Good doesn't need evil. We'd be just as well rid of it."

If we must place the century in a time capsule, there are better candidates for Person of the Century than its greatest criminal. The large characters, heroes and villains alike, do set the scales on which we balance progress. Evil may be a powerful force, a seductive idea, but is it more powerful than genius, creativity, courage or generosity? The century has offered characters who stretched our understanding and faith in those qualities as well. The heroes not only defeated Hitler; they provided our lasting inspiration as well. "Just as Hitler made us believe we hadn't yet sounded the depths," notes Rosenbaum, "maybe Martin Luther King Jr. and the great artists of the century, like Nabokov, help us believe there are still heights we haven't found." ∎

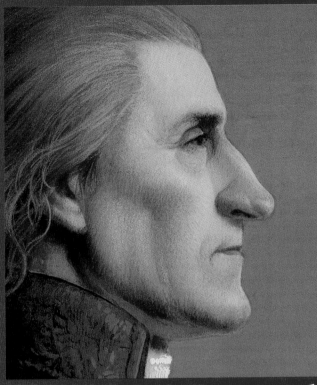

The Most Important People of the
Millennium

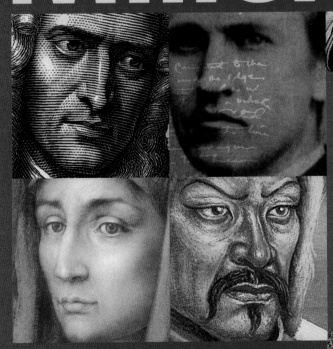

William (c. 1027-1087)

the Conqueror

The Norman took what he believed was his —England —and pioneered state bureaucracy amid Europe's chaos

By DAVID VAN BIEMA

He was, contemporaries advise us, "great in body ... but not ungainly." He had a harsh voice, but his speech was always appropriate. His chroniclers lauded his ability to "appraise the true significance of events" and make good "the fickle promises of fortune." They also remarked that he was "too relentless to care, though all might hate him." William the Conqueror was a man—or, more important, a monarch—for a new age.

Europe entered the century as a study in disintegrated empire. Rome had long since fallen. Charlemagne had briefly laid claim to its authority, but his heirs could not sustain a continent-wide order. Christendom was a Babel of weak and squabbling kings, aristocrats whose holdings sometimes exceeded those of royalty, and a church that would spawn two competing Popes.

It was a chaotic era, and William of Normandy, born around 1027, was the child of chaos. The illegitimate son of Robert, Duke of Normandy, he was known for most of his life as William the Bastard. Robert eventually recognized him, but only as he departed on a fatal pilgrimage to the Holy Land, leaving his seven-year-old a target for usurping barons. One by one, William's guardians and advisers were cut down. The boy escaped assassination only by a desperate flight to his mother's estate.

REMAINS OF THE DAY

PET OF THE MILLENNIUM
Pyramid carvings show images of the forebears of chihuahuas, (called *techichis*). The canines became top dogs in the Yucatán and other large tracts of Mexico when their masters, the Toltecs, conquered the area— about 1,000 years "B.C." (that is, Before the Chalupa).

BEST NOVEL
The Tale of Genji by the Lady Murasaki chronicled the amorous exploits of a prince in Kyoto, including trysts with his stepmother, the Empress of Japan (she bears his son, who inherits the throne). *Genji*, in a racy version in modern language by a 77-year-old Buddhist nun, is a best seller today.

(c. 1138-1193)

Saladin

The Kurdish adventurer proved to the Crusaders that God had no trouble favoring an "infidel"

By DAVID VAN BIEMA

When Dante Alighieri compiled his great medieval *Who's Who* of heroes and villains, the *Divine Comedy*, the highest a non-Christian could climb was Limbo. Ancient pagans had to be virtuous indeed to warrant inclusion: the residents included Homer, Caesar, Plato and Dante's guide, Vergil. But perhaps the most surprising entry in Dante's catalog of "great-hearted souls" was an unexpected figure "solitary, set apart."

That figure was Saladin. It is testament to his extraordinary stature in the Middle Ages that not only was Saladin the sole "modern" mentioned—he had been dead barely 100 years when Dante wrote—but also that a man who had made his name successfully battling Christianity would be lionized by the author of perhaps the most Christ-centered verse ever penned.

When Salah al-Din Yusuf ibn Ayyub was born in 1138 to a family of Kurdish adventurers in the (now Iraqi) town of Takrit, Islam was a confusion of squabbling warlords living under a Christian shadow. A generation before, European Crusaders had conquered Jerusalem, massacring its Muslim and Jewish inhabitants. The Franks, as they were called, then occupied four militarily aggressive states in the Holy Land. The powerful Syrian

REMAINS OF THE DAY

BEST LITERARY INNOVATION
The poet of Arthurian chivalry Chrétien de Troyes was the first to describe a mysterious "grail"—a beautiful vessel that, together with a lance, forms part of a strange procession witnessed by the knight Perceval, who cannot fathom its meaning. Later writers would insist this "Holy Grail" was the cup of the Last Supper, in which Joseph of Arimathea preserved the blood of the crucified Jesus.

BEST NEW SCHOOL
In 1117 history recorded the first "master" at a place where the Thames was narrow enough for oxen to ford. Oxford soon saw French theologians on lecture tour. By the 14th century, the Oxford colleges—which formed a university under a guild of masters—were as influential as those of Paris.

leader Nur al-Din predicted that expelling the European invaders would require a holy war of the sort that had propelled Islam's first great wave of expansion half a millennium earlier, but given the treacherous regional crosscurrents, such a united front seemed highly unlikely.

Saladin finally got his chance with the death, in 1169, of his uncle Shirkuh, a one-eyed, overweight brawler in Nur al-Din's service who had become the de facto leader of Egypt. A seasoned warrior despite his small stature and frailty, Saladin still had a tough hand to play. He was a Kurd (even then a drawback in Middle Eastern politics), and he was from Syria, a Sunni state, trying to rule Egypt, a Shi'ite country. But a masterly 17-year campaign employing diplomacy, the sword and great good fortune made him lord of Egypt, Syria and much of Mesopotamia. The lands bracketed the Crusader states, and their combined might at last made plausible Nur al-Din's dream of a Muslim-Christian showdown.

THAT ENCOUNTER TOOK PLACE near Hattin, within sight of the Golan Heights. Saladin had assembled a pan-Islamic force of 12,000 cavalry near Lake Tiberias. The Christians were lured on a long July march across Galilee's parched Plain of Lubiya. Saladin had the right bait—he had besieged the lakeside town in which a knight's wife was staying—and the Crusader force, frying in heavy armor and unable to fight its way to the water, was overwhelmed by the Muslims. When the Christian knights retreated to the coastal fortress of Tyre, Saladin turned his army inland. Jerusalem withstood him for less than two weeks. In stark contrast to the earlier Crusader bloodbath, his occupiers

> ❝ Facing me there, on the enameled green, great-hearted souls were shown to me ... Hector and Aeneas, Caesar in his armor, falcon-eyed ... and solitary, set apart, Saladin. ❞
>
> **DANTE, *INFERNO***

neither murdered nor looted. "Christians everywhere will remember the kindness we have bestowed upon them," Saladin predicted—and he was correct.

In a shocked Europe, the Pope immediately called a Third Crusade. And although Richard the Lion-Hearted bested Saladin in battle after battle, the English royal could not wrest the Holy City from the Muslims, and Richard returned to Europe. The city, always Islam's third holiest site, became even more central to the faithful. Saladin's family ruled less than 60 years longer, but his style of administration and his humane application of justice to both war and governance influenced Arab rulers for centuries. His tolerance was exemplary. He allowed Christian pilgrims in Jerusalem after its fall. The great Jewish sage Maimonides was his physician. The man who won fame as a warrior and diplomat was also a great patron of Islamic culture. He founded colleges and mosques, courted scholars and preachers, commissioned writings on sacred subjects. Woven into chivalric legend as the worthy foeman, Saladin, scimitar flashing or compassionately sheathed, galloped from Dante into romances by Sir Walter Scott and eventually into young-adult books that ship today in 24 hours through Amazon.com.

Both Iraq's Saddam Hussein and Syria's Hafez Assad have at times invoked Saladin against Israel, the new "crusader." However, they seem unlikely to attain either the military triumph that safeguarded one world or the nobility of mind that endeared him to another. ■

WORST BRUSH-OFF
The Emperor Huizong of China's Song dynasty was a gifted calligrapher and painter. But his skills as potentate were wanting. In 1127 invaders conquered most of northern China, taking Huizong prisoner. He died an exile in Manchuria.

BEST GUIDANCE TOOL
The mariner's compass was used by the Chinese well before 1050, the year the instrument made its appearance in European ships plying Mediterranean waters.

Warriors of the Will

In an age of rigid heirarchies, uncompromising individuals disdained the rules and took command of their destinies

Eleanor of Aquitaine (c. 1122-1204)
Insider of the Century

She was the most powerful woman at a time when the "lesser sex" was supposed to be seen, not heard. But how could anyone suppress Eleanor? She was

heiress to the largest and richest fiefdom in France, then Queen of France, then Queen of England. She went on crusade and was rumored, ridiculously, to have planned to elope with Saladin (he would have been about 11). It was her idea to leave the French King, not the other way around. And when she brought her inheritance to her next husband, Henry II, she set in motion hundreds of years of Anglo-French wars. With her sons she staged an unsuccessful rebellion against her unfaithful husband; then she became the most celebrated political prisoner of the age, begetter of a cult of romance and the object of troubadors' plaintive songs. She outlived Henry, who was more than 10 years her junior, to place two sons—first her favorite, Richard the Lion-Hearted, then John—on the English throne.

Yoritomo (1147-1199)
Generalissimo of the Century

He took the ancient but honorary title of shogun (short for *sei-i-tai-shogun*, or great barbarian-subduing general) and made it the most potent rank in a samurai government that eclipsed all pretense to worldly power by the imperial family. Such regimes would dominate Japan for seven centuries. Exiled after his father's execution, Yoritomo found revenge in exterminating a rival clan and seeing a child Emperor drowned. Overcoming the aristocrats from Kyoto—the Emperor's capital—he set up his own capital in the east, where he had been exiled, making the area around modern-day Tokyo a new center of power.

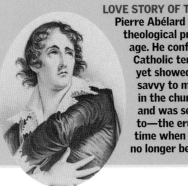

LOVE STORY OF THE CENTURY
Pierre Abélard was the theological provocateur of the age. He confounded Roman Catholic tenets with reason, yet showed enough political savvy to merit advancement in the church. But he loved—and was secretly married to—the erudite Héloïse at a time when married men could no longer be priests. After a melodrama that shifted from bedroom to birthing chamber to convent, Abélard was set upon by enemies in 1119 and castrated. He became a monk; she a nun. But they still corresponded. "Sweeter to me is ever the word friend, or, if thou be not ashamed, concubine or whore," reads one of her purported letters. "What queen or powerful lady did not envy me my joys and my bed?"

(c. 1167-1227)
Genghis Khan

The conqueror swept through Asia, setting in motion forces more powerful than the sword

BY HOWARD CHUA-EOAN

Temujin was born clutching a blood clot the size of a knucklebone. His name was war booty, taken from a captive rival by his proud warrior father and tacked on like a medal to his firstborn son. But history echoes with another of his names, a title Temujin would receive 39 years later. In 1206, by acclamation of all the Mongols, he became Genghis Khan, the "Oceanic Ruler" who in the next two decades would father an empire that rolled across Eurasia, linking the Pacific Ocean to the Black Sea as it amassed kingdoms as loot and nations as slaves. The legacy of Genghis Khan is as terrifying as genocide and as dreadful as the plague. But this is the paradox: its romance is as seductive as Xanadu and its impact on history as momentous as the discovery of America.

His forebears were a blue-gray wolf and a fallow doe. The coupling of these legendary ancestors, of predator and prey, produced a human being from whom all Mongols would claim descent. But such fantastical beginnings did little to ease the early life of the world conqueror—unless the myth was an omen for living like a wild animal in the steppes around Lake Baikal. His father Yesugei was poisoned by enemies and his widowed mother Hoelun chased away from their tribe with her brood, including her eldest, nine-year-old Temujin. The

REMAINS OF THE DAY

BEST PUBLISHING MEDIUM
Arabs brought paper to Spain and soon it entered Italy; finally Europe had a cheap alternative to vellum and parchment. (It took the skins of 80 lambs to create a 200-page parchment manuscript.) Block printing arrived in Europe around the same time, perhaps brought by merchants and bureaucrats of the expanding Mongol Empire.

BEST PIECE OF ETIQUETTE
The fork slowly—very slowly—began to win acceptance in Europe. It had caused a scandal when a Venetian Doge's Byzantine wife used it in the 11th century. Such "excessive delicacy," said St. Peter Damian, caused her body to "rot away." For centuries, the utensil remained an affectation. As late as the 1800s, Neapolitans were still eating spaghetti by hand, and the Viennese were eating their cake with knives.

outcasts ate field mice and marmots even as they fought off thieves out for their horses, the most precious of nomad property. Bitterness cultivated a heart of iron. After a half-brother grabbed a fish he had hooked, Temujin killed the offending sibling in a hail of arrows. He never showed remorse. His mother was furious at the waste of a potential soldier in the revenge she envisioned. "We have no one to fight with us," she hectored, "except our own shadows."

Out of the shadows, however, Temujin would create a nation and the most disciplined fighting force on the planet. First, he escaped the wild by making a good marriage. That alliance would lead to more critical alliances as Temujin learned to ply diplomacy and a ruthless militancy. Soon, his almost supernatural generalship would win him fiercely loyal followers, enough to offset a multiplicity of traitors and false friends. He vanquished the fractious tribalism of the Mongols by dispersing clansmen among regiments in an army that used death as discipline and looting as reward. Conquered peoples were divided among the armies, swelling the ranks of fighters. Similarly, the technology of the conquered cultures was absorbed like more booty and enrolled in an intercultural war of conquest. Thus the elaborate catapults developed in Central Asia were deployed against the stout walls of China. And the explosive bombs and rockets pioneered in China were later put to use in Mesopotamia and Europe.

Terror, however, was the Khan's greatest weapon. Cities that resisted the Mongols were made examples of. Their populations were slaughtered indiscriminately and the survivors marched before the Mongol armies to buffer counterattacks: human shields nearly eight centuries before Saddam Hussein. Cities that surrendered without a fight were spared, their citizens merely enslaved.

The great Khan's strategies led to the subjugation of the

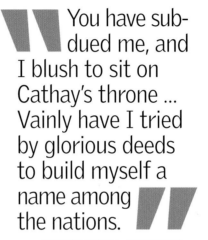

> **"** You have subdued me, and I blush to sit on Cathay's throne ... Vainly have I tried by glorious deeds to build myself a name among the nations. **"**
>
> **GENGHIS KHAN in VOLTAIRE'S**
> ***ORPHELIN DE LA CHINE***

advanced civilizations of northern China and Persia. His sons and grandsons would extend the empire. Batu would command armies that struck deep into Russia and swept through Poland into Germany, Hungary and the Balkans. Kublai Khan, who would later build his stately pleasure dome in the city of Shangtu (Coleridge's Xanadu), conquered southern China and Burma. His brother Hulegu would not only destroy Baghdad but also devastate its irrigation network. Mesopotamia has never fully recovered.

The immense wealth of the Mongol empire and the suddenly free passage from west to east attracted merchants and adventurers, whose goods and tales would change the world. Marco Polo's stories became the dreams of Christopher Columbus. The quest for a passage to Cathay, the medieval name for northern China, would propel countless explorers to serendipitous discoveries in America. (In 1634, for example, the Frenchman Jean Nicolet left Quebec in search of China and discovered Green Bay, Wis.) In similar fashion, Franciscan missionary diplomats sent by the Pope to seek an alliance with the Khan against Islam brought back a black powder to a fellow Franciscan, the Oxford scientist Roger Bacon, the first European to write about gunpowder.

However, the most indirect, though by no means benign, gift of the Khan was the plague. Originating in the jungles of southern China and Burma, bubonic plague traveled with Mongol armies and then from caravan to caravan till it reached the Crimea in 1347. From there it would take the lives of a third of all Europeans. Result: bereft of labor and talent, the fledgling nation-states were pressed to maximize tax collection, bureaucracy and state control of the force of arms, leading to the heightened competitiveness of the West just as Europe's ships sailed for the riches of a distant empire. The rest is the history of another world conquest. ∎

HOT NEW DYNASTY
In 1273 the Swiss-German Count Rudolf became the first Habsburg to wear a crown, that of the Holy Roman Empire. By the 20th century, the family had ruled, at one time or another, Germany, Spain, Portugal, the Netherlands, Switzerland, large portions of Italy, Austria, Hungary, parts of the Balkans, vast sections of Latin America and the Philippines.

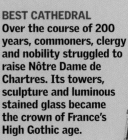
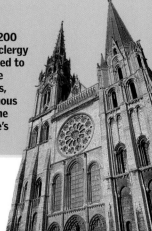

BEST CATHEDRAL
Over the course of 200 years, commoners, clergy and nobility struggled to raise Nôtre Dame de Chartres. Its towers, sculpture and luminous stained glass became the crown of France's High Gothic age.

In Love with the Eternal

From the world-embracing spirituality of an Italian friar to the visions of an Islamic seer, it was an age of grace

Francis of Assisi (c. 1182-1226)
Saint of the Century

He was born into a prospering class at a time of European plenty. To encourage riches, the church preached industry, a get-ahead attitude that had little regard for outcasts, for lepers, for the poor. The revelation of Francis was that poverty was holy and that the spirit approached God when in want. He kissed lepers and gave away his possessions. He preached naked from the pulpit. The church saw his ideals as a dangerous communism and undermined him by co-opting his Friars Minor, which gorged itself with power after his death. Yet Francis changed the face of sanctity: heaven was now in the face of the abject and in the horror of disease. Lenin said if there had been 10 of Francis, there would have been no need for revolution. A saint for all seasons and all ages, Francis retained his appeal in the 20th century as the subject of songs, films and the books of such writers as Nikos Kazantzakis.

Jalal ad-Din Rumi (1207-73)
Mystic of the Century

God is avenger; god is king. But Rumi, more than any other mystic in any other faith, dared to reveal God as beauty. He heard the divine in music; he saw it in the sun; he felt it in his companions. It was not an era that encouraged such perceptions. Rumi was a refugee from the onslaught of the Mongols, finding safe harbor in the cosmopolitan city of Iconium (now Konya, in modern-day Turkey), thousands of miles from his birthplace in Afghanistan. Yet he said that though people fled the Mongols, he served the Creator of the Mongols. No other poet found such ecstasy in daily wonderment, in song, in vision, in wine, in dance and most important, in friendship. His poems (the Persian Koran, some say) reverberate to this day in Iran, Turkey and Pakistan. They border on the erotic, with water seeking the thirsty as much as thirst seeks quenching, with the music of the reed flute longing for the reedbed from which the instrument had been plucked. The Sufi sect of the whirling dervishes dances to his rhythm; New Age meditations echo his songs.

BETTER THAN NOTHING
In 1202 the zero finally got a firm foothold in Europe. For two centuries, the system of numerals that included zero had been toyed with but rejected by Christian clerics as part of the "infidel" numerical system of the Arabs, who adopted it from Hindu savants. By the 16th century, zero had transfigured the art of European calculation.

BEST AGREEMENT
English barons, allied with the clergy and merchants, wanted to protect their interests from a voracious, incompetent King. In 1215 they showed enough force to intimidate John I into agreeing that royal authority was not equivalent to arbitrary power and that taxation should benefit the kingdom, not the King. John's seals on the document (above) were a first step in constitutional government—the Magna Carta.

With his brush, the severity of religious icons melted into warm humanity, and the face of the God-like became the face of man

By JOHANNA McGEARY

(c. 1267-1337)

Giotto

Put yourself back to a time before true mirrors. In Europe the art of painting had been lost to the ruthless destruction of barbarians. No Western man could see an authentic likeness of humankind rendered on a wall because no artist knew how to draw one. The pictures that adorned medieval churches—there was no secular painting—eschewed reality for decoration or dogma. Gilt-bedizened Madonnas with flat, staring eyes holding outsize infant Christs bespoke not man but the supernatural mystery of the faith.

Then came Giotto. He was an artisan like countless others of the age, though he possessed something his predecessors and contemporaries did not: an inner eye that could see how human figures could be brought to life on a wall. He replaced golden backdrops with the hills, meadows and houses familiar to 14th century Italians. In those earthly settings he placed three-dimensional Christs and Virgins, saints and sinners, painted as ordinary humans invested with natural emotions. His sweetly weary Madonna locks eyes with the observer as she swaddles a baby-size Jesus.

We who are jaded by the unnatural deconstructions of 20th century art cannot easily imagine the electric impact Giotto made by painting natural human figures that reached out of their frames to

REMAINS OF THE DAY

BEST WORLDLY EPIC
A round of tales told by 30 or so pilgrims off to the shrine of St. Thomas Becket, Geoffrey Chaucer's *Canterbury Tales* brims with fully fleshed characters like the Wife of Bath and the Pardoner that modern pilgrims will still find provocative. Their bluster about the role of the sexes in marriage and their speculation about self and death prefigure Shakespeare.

communicate directly with the observer. This was not simply a marvel in a superstitious age but also the artistic birth of the Renaissance. Giotto fathered a radical revolution of startling genius that set the course of Western art for the next 600 years.

Little is known of the life and development of Giotto di Bondone, born around 1267 to peasants in the bucolic val-

> **[Giotto was] the best painter in the world ... [he resurrected] that art which had been buried for centuries by the errors of some who painted more to please the eyes of the ignorant than the intellect of the wise.**
>
> BOCCACCIO, *THE DECAMERON*

leys outside Florence. Legend says the country boy tending his flocks was discovered by the painter Cimabue, who saw him draw a fine sheep upon a rock. A more likely tale has him haunting Cimabue's Florentine *bottega* until the painter made him an apprentice. There Giotto absorbed his mentor's strength of drawing and sense of drama, but nature was his true teacher. He divined how to depict, with brush and pigment, the human body according to the prescription of St. Francis: "Your God is of your flesh. He lives in your nearest neighbor, in every man." And he surpassed his master: even Dante, who had pronounced Cimabue without equal, declared that "now Giotto has the acclaim."

And so Giotto painted his Bible stories and tales of saints across the cathedral walls of Italy. His patrons included the Pope; Enrico Scrovegni, the richest and most influential citizen of Padua; the king of Naples; and Azzone Visconti, the Signore of Milan.

Yet though Giotto's influence has persisted, his works have fallen prey to time: we can see his brilliance today in only a bare handful of surviving documented works. The famous 28 scenes of St. Francis' life adorning the Upper Church in Assisi—to most of us the embodiment of the artist's work—are of hotly disputed authorship. Yet many experts still believe no other known hand could have created the economical drama, narrative power and intense depiction of human emotion that mark the best of them.

There is no dispute concerning another great trove of masterpieces: Giotto's genius is definitively preserved in Padua in a small chapel completely decorated in powerful renditions of the life of the Virgin Mary and the Passion of Christ. In each of the panels a number of simple figures anchored in the foreground vividly act out the joy, grief, fear and pity of the Christian story.

Giotto's gift lay in transforming the viewer into a participant, in erasing the immense gulf between the personal and the divine: people felt as if they could touch these holy figures that Ruskin, in a playful mood, once called "Mama, Papa and the Baby."

By breaking through the stilted conventions of medieval art, bringing his neighbors into direct communion with the sacred, Giotto single-handedly elevated painting from the service of symbolism to the mirror of mankind. ■

BEST OTHERWORLDLY EPIC
Midway into the tumult of Renaissance Florence, Dante Alighieri stopped to survey heaven, earth, hell and history—with himself and his trials at the psychological center. Consigning the great and the small to *Inferno, Purgatorio* or *Paradiso*, his *Divine Comedy* is a masterpiece of the Christian imagination and evidence that literature can be a potent weapon against the real world.

BEST TRAVELOGUE
Marco Polo's *Travels*, probably dictated in 1298, is described by China scholar Jonathan Spence as "a combination of verifiable fact, random information posing as statistics, exaggeration, make believe, ... and a certain amount of outright fabrication." However imprecise, the book captivated Western minds in the 14th century, tantalizing Europe with the notion of an advanced civilization in China.

When Warlords Held Sway

A pair of ruthless warriors established empires that advanced culture—on foundations of terror and woe

Zhu Yuanzhang (1328-1398)
Dictator of the Century

Orphaned, homeless, his face scarred by disease, Zhu survived countless dangers to become a warlord, chase out the descendants of Genghis Khan and

become the first Emperor of the Ming dynasty in China. Pained by the memory of his rootlessness, he decreed that peasants could not venture far from the villages of their birth. The demographic concentration that resulted led to an agricultural bonanza, with surpluses creating purchasing power and huge new internal markets for commodities, which in turn created textile, porcelain and other manufacturing centers. Such productivity would later attract foreigners: Spain extracted huge amounts of silver from its South American colonies to pay for Chinese goods. By the 16th century, ordinary Chinese were the most prosperous inhabitants of the planet. All because of a homeless man.

Tamerlane (1336-1405)
Terror of the Century

The English, who lived far beyond his conquests, knew to tremble at the name. "The scourge of God," Christopher Marlowe quailed nearly 200 years after the death of the military genius from Samarkand. When the city of Isfahan defied him, Tamerlane slaughtered 70,000 of its inhabitants and raised a pyramid of heads. Christendom thought the haughty Ottoman Sultan Bayezit was threat enough. Then Bayezit insulted Tamerlane. Routed in battle, the Sultan was locked in a cage and driven mad, then bashed his brains out on the bars. More accurately known as Timur-i-Leng ("Timur the Lame," for an arrow wound to the heel), the warlord loved beauty as much as war and turned Samarkand into a wonder of the world. There his name is still spoken of with pride

and awe. He left a curse for anyone who dared disturb his tomb. Locals shake their head telling of the day the Soviets broke in to examine his skull. On that day the cataclysmic Nazi invasion of Russia began. Tamerlane, it turned out, was also the scourge of the godless.

MOST WATCHED INNOVATION
A revolutionary new sense of time slowly took over Europe as mechanical clocks began to measure equal hours in town plazas and squares. Communities, however, set their clocks their own way, depending on when the sun rose or set on their horizon. And while clocks struck the hour, few had minute hands. Clock resettings were soon transformed into colorful civic ceremonies.

WORST BIOLOGICAL AGENT
No King, no Pope, no war would affect Europe like the Black Death, which began to sweep through in 1347. At least a third of the Continent's population perished, and kingdoms were gripped by labor shortages. Scientists and historians believe the culprit was the bacillus *Pasteurella pestis,* which spread from southern Asia to Europe via rats and fleas along trade routes.

(c. 1395-1468)

Johann Gutenberg

The obscure German printer's innovation kindled religious reforms and an ongoing information revolution

By PAUL GRAY

The French peasant girl who rallied her country's dispirited troops against the occupying English forces; the Turkish ruler who conquered Constantinople and enlarged what would become the millennium's most durable empire; the Italian navigator who sailed the ocean blue in 1492. Joan of Arc, Sultan Mehmet II and Christopher Columbus indisputably made lasting history. But it was one of their 15th century contemporaries who created a revolutionary way to spread not only their names and deeds but the sum total of human knowledge around the globe.

Johann Gutenberg was born of well-to-do parents in the Archbishopric of Mainz, Germany. Details of his life, early as well as late, are sketchy, but he apparently trained as a goldsmith and/or gem cutter and then became a partner in a printing shop in Strasbourg. When Gutenberg entered it, printing was a slow and laborious business. Each new page required the creation of a new printing form, usually an incised block of wood. He began looking for ways to make metal casts of the individual letters of the alphabet. The advantages of such a method were obvious, or must have been to Gutenberg. Equipped with a sufficient supply of metal letters, a printer could use and reuse them in any order required, running off not just handbills and brief documents but a

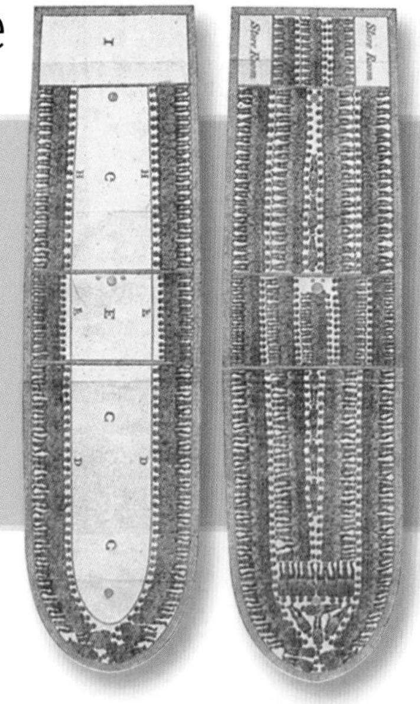

REMAINS OF THE DAY

WORST MISSED OPPORTUNITY
From 1405 to 1433, the eunuch Zheng commanded seven voyages that projected Chinese power throughout Asia and East Africa. The massive armada dwarfed all navies. But the Ming Emperor took to isolationism, and the voyages ended. Then the Europeans came.

WORST ENTERPRISE
In 1444 a Portuguese explorer-entrepreneur purchased 230 Africans and began the mechanics of the slave trade that would later take millions across the Atlantic. By 1511 the Dominican monk Bartolomé de las Casas began lobbying the Spanish King for African slaves to be sent to America, arguing that Native American populations needed relief from mistreatment by colonizers. Between 1500 and 1870, some 12 million Africans were taken to the Americas.

theoretically infinite number of individual pages. There were technical obstacles to overcome, including the discovery of an alloy that would melt at moderate temperatures, so that it could be poured into letter molds, and of an ink that would crisply transfer impressions from metal to paper. And to make these impressions, Gutenberg hit upon the idea of adapting a wine press for new uses.

By the time he was back in Mainz in 1448, Gutenberg had ironed out enough of these problems to persuade Johann Fust, a goldsmith and lawyer, to invest heavily in his new printing shop. Exactly what happened behind Gutenberg's closed doors during the next few years remains unknown. But in 1455 visitors to the Frankfurt Trade Fair reported having seen sections of a Latin Bible with two columns of 42 lines apiece printed—printed—on each page. The completed book appeared about a year later; it did not bear its printer's name, but it eventually became known as the Gutenberg Bible.

> ## He who first shortened the labor of copyists by device of movable types ... was creating a whole new democratic world.
>
> **THOMAS CARLYLE**

IT WAS A REVELATION, AT LEAST TO WESTERN EYES: multiple copies of an entire volume produced by mechanical means. True, printing from movable type had been performed in Asia, but thousands of ideograms made the widespread use of the technique impractical. Gutenberg, who apparently knew nothing of the Asian innovations, was blessed not only with an inventive mind but also with a phonetic alphabet and its manageable cast of characters.

Shortly before his completed bible was released, Gutenberg was forced to turn over his shop and at least some of his equipment to his creditor Fust, who carried on the work. His monopoly on Gutenberg's methods did not last long. Presses adapted to print from movable type rapidly spread across Europe. By 1500—within five decades—an estimated 30,000 titles had been published.

And that was only the beginning of a tide of print that has been rising ever since. We can hardly imagine a world without an abundance of printed matter, and thus we take for granted an invention that produced astonishing consequences. Early printed books resembled, in their appearance as well as their content, the laboriously hand-copied manuscripts they replaced. The dissemination of the writings of Greek and Roman authors led to a revival of the classical learning that spurred the Renaissance. Printed religious texts put the word of God directly into the hands of lay readers. The removal of ecclesiastical middlemen from the relationship between the individual and divine Scripture inspired a new emphasis on personal salvation that helped fuel the Protestant Reformation.

Before the advent of print, the ability to read was useful mainly to the élite and the highly trained scribes who managed their affairs. Affordable books made literacy a crucial skill and an unprecedented means of social advancement to those who acquired it. As printed words undermined old barriers, established hierarchies began to crumble. Books were the world's first mass-produced—and mass-consumed items. Above all, printing was the greatest extension of human consciousness ever created. Its work isn't over: the 500-year-old information revolution continues on the Internet. And thanks to a German printer who wanted a more efficient way to do business, you can look that up. ∎

BEST PERSPECTIVE
It's perspective itself. The ancient Romans may have had some idea of it, but it was Renaissance architects like Filippo Brunelleschi, designer of Il Duomo, the dome of the great cathedral of Florence, who became the true masters of this most deceptive of arts, inspiring a future filled with Botticellis, Leonardos, Raphaels, Michelangelos et al.

BEST SPEEDBOAT
Prince Henry the Navigator of Portugal organized a naval academy of engineers, mapmakers and ship's pilots. Borrowing from Arab vessels, they designed the first caravels. Propelled by lateen rigging, the three-masted ships were fast and tacked into the wind.

Visions of Glory

A navigator who became a laughingstock and a young girl who was burned as a witch shaped the course of history

Christopher Columbus (1451-1506)
Explorer of the Century

After his death, Columbus became a laughingstock. Vasco da Gama got to the real Indies; Magellan crossed two oceans; Cortés conquered Mexico. But Columbus couldn't even handle a start-up colony in the Caribbean. It was the people who followed him to the new world he discovered who made him a perpetual paradox, a symbol of pride and contention, an emblem in their search for identity.

The citizens of the U.S. took to naming places Columbia, and he became the ethnic icon of millions of immigrants. Others dubbed him the "Civilizer," but that rubbed many the wrong way. Wasn't he the harbinger of disaster for native cultures and thus "the deadest of dead white males"? The debate goes on. Columbus was bullheaded and wrong-minded about finding China across the sea. But the navigator declared he would never be forgotten, and as of 500 years later, he's right.

Joan of Arc (c. 1412-1431)
Soldier of the Century

Voices came to the 17-year-old farm girl and told her that the uncrowned King, whom many believed illegitimate, was worth fighting and dying for. So Joan offered her services to Charles, declaring she could lift the siege of Orléans. She then led and inspired 10,000 men to do just that, defeating the English who occupied most of France. She said that the King must be anointed and crowned at Reims.

And so he was, on July 17, 1429. Then Joan's campaign faltered. She was captured by the enemy, convicted of sorcery and burned at the stake. But until the end, she clung to her voices. France fought on, and on July 17, 1453, Charles' armies ended English rule. Economic historians say the railroads made France a nation. Perhaps. But Joan made France want to be one.

BEST BLESSING IN DISGUISE
Constantinople and the remnant of the Byzantine Empire fell to the Ottoman Sultan Mehmet II in 1453. Far from declining, the city became the resplendent capital of the powerful Turks. And, fore-shadowing Starbucks, the conquerors opened coffeehouses throughout the city.

WORST JUDICIAL FORM
Kafkaesque before Kafka was cool, Henry VII of England introduced the prototype of the Star Chamber. The procedure granted defendants no right to know the names of their accusers.

Queen Elizabeth I

(1533-1603)

The goddess of the Reformation defeated Europe's greatest power and set Britain on its epic journey to empire

By JOHANNA McGEARY

First feminist. First spinmeister. Megawatt celeb. So might our age judge her. To 16th century England, Elizabeth embodied the original feminine mystique: goddess Gloriana; Virgin Queen; finally and enduringly, Good Queen Bess. The most remarkable woman ruler in history can claim few traditional princely achievements, yet she gave her name to an age. Hers was a prodigious political success story built on the power of personality: the Queen as star. A woman so strong, a politician so skillful, a monarch so magnetic that she impressed herself indelibly on the minds of her people and reshaped the fate of England. She brought her country safely through the Reformation, inspired a cultural Renaissance and united a tiny, fragmented island into a nation of global reach.

Elizabeth was born unpropitiously into a man's world and a man's role. Desiring a son, Elizabeth's father Henry VIII divorced his first wife and broke with the Roman Catholic Church to marry Anne Boleyn. When Anne bore him a girl, he ordered his wife beheaded and the child princess declared a bastard. Elizabeth grew up in loneliness and danger, learning the urgency of keeping her balance on England's quivering political tightrope. She was lucky to receive a boy's rigorous education, tutored by distinguished scholars in the classics, history, philosophy, languages and

REMAINS OF THE DAY

BEST ENLIGHTENED DESPOT
The third ruler of the Islamic Mughal dynasty, Akbar ruled an immense empire in India that included millions more Hindus than Muslims. Not only did the warrior King marry Hindu princesses, but he lifted religious taxes on Hindus and built Hindu temples.

BEST IMPORT
Christopher Columbus brought the seeds of the cacao plant (backdrop at left) to Spain in 1502. But no one knew what to do with the bitter bean until Hernando Cortés was served a goblet of liquid *xocoatl* (bitter water) at the court of the Aztec ruler Montezuma in 1519. With some sweetening, Spain had a hit with chocolate and kept the recipe a national secret for almost a century.

theology. She was serious and quick witted. "Her mind has no womanly weakness," said her teacher Roger Ascham, but she equally loved music, dancing and gaiety. During the bloody reigns of her Protestant half brother and zealously Catholic half sister, Elizabeth needed all her poise, discipline and political acumen just to survive.

THE BELLS OF LONDON TOLLED JOYOUSLY ON NOV. 17, 1558, when Elizabeth ascended the throne. She made her coronation the first in a lifetime of scintillant spectacles, visual manifestations of her rule. As she walked down the carpet in Westminster Abbey, citizens scrambled behind her to cut off pieces. Her power started as a grand illusion, but it was prophetic.

With her political and personal security threatened from beginning to end, Elizabeth needed all her courage, cunning and caution to reign. She took the throne of a poor, isolated and deeply humiliated country. As a Queen, she faced special problems of marriage and succession, religious division, domestic discontent and foreign threats. Her Church of England restored the country firmly to Protestantism, yet she allowed Catholics freedom of worship, easing the bitter religious strife of Mary's reign.

Elizabeth spent a lifetime contending with the issue of marriage and royal heirs and the challenges raised by men who would steal her scepter. Marriage is what 16th century women were for, and Queens needed heirs. She engaged in the most manipulative, interminable courtships, driven not by love but by politics—though she was tirelessly fond of suitors. Leading a weak country in need of foreign allies, she brilliantly played the diplomatic marriage game: at one time she kept a French royal dangling farcically for nearly 10 years. Always she concluded that the perils of matrimony exceeded the benefits. She courted English suitors too, for both pleasure and politics. Yet when favorite Robert Dudley, Earl of Leicester, pressed too hard, she retorted, "I will have here but one mistress and no master." She did not wed because she refused to give up any power. "Beggarwoman and single far rather than Queen and married," she once said.

Playing on the cult of the Virgin Mary, she drew devotion to herself, virgin mother of the nation. "This shall be for me sufficient," she told Parliament, "that a marble stone shall declare that a Queen, having reigned such a time, lived and died a virgin." She was, in the end, married to England.

Elizabeth's way of escaping gender restrictions and defining herself as a legitimate ruler lay in consummate imagemaking. She stage-managed her personality cult. She dressed to kill, glittering with jewels in wondrous costumes to bedazzle her subjects. She went on royal progresses—the equivalent of photo-ops—to show off and get to know her people. She had the common touch, able to rouse a crowd or charm a citizen. She had flattering portraits painted and copies widely distributed. She encouraged balladeers to pen propagandistic songs. Her marvelous mythmaking machinery cultivated a mystic bond with the English people. "We all loved her," wrote her godson Sir John Harington, "for she said she loved us."

Notoriously parsimonious—except for her own fashions—Elizabeth hated war for its costly wastefulness, yet embroiled England ineffectually in the long Continental struggles of the Counter-Reformation. When the Catholic threat of Spain reached its apogee in 1588, her penny pinching nearly cost England its independence before luck and the skill of her sailors defeated the Spanish armada. Yet at the moment of imminent invasion, she dressed in a silver breastplate to address her troops and imbue them with her dauntless courage. "I know I have the body of a weak and feeble woman," Elizabeth said, "but I have the heart and stomach of a King, and a King of England too." Her countrymen gloried in her victory, transforming the battle into an act of national consciousness that gave birth to nearly four centuries of patriotic imperialism. She spawned England's empire, chartering seven companies—including the East India—to plunder and colonize in the name of trade.

She was a larger-than-life royal with a genius for rule who came to embody England as had few before her. The new spirit emanating from so brilliant a sovereign inspired a flowering of enduring literature, music, drama, poetry. Determinedly molding herself into the image of a mighty prince, she made of England a true and mighty nation. ■

BEST (NEAR) FACE-OFF
Michelangelo had just completed his *David*, left, and Leonardo was working on the *Mona Lisa* when both were commissioned to paint murals at the Palazzo Vecchio in Florence. Hoping to show up his rival, Michelangelo began a 288-sq.-ft. sketch. But the Pope ordered the sculptor to Rome, foiling the matchup.

WORST ORGY
Raphael, left, was, along with Leonardo and Michelangelo, one of the trinity of the High Renaissance. His death in 1520 is still a mystery, but an artist-chronicler of the time, Giorgio Vasari, believes it was the result of the painter's propensity for exhausting sexual debauchery.

When Worldviews Collide

A pair of nonconformists shattered ancient assumptions of religion and cosmology, unleashing an era of change

Martin Luther (1483-1546)
Ideologue of the Century

In the 16th century, if those in power disagreed with your writing, they usually burned it. If you kept issuing the same, they burned you. Martin Luther,

brave and cantankerous soul, kept writing, turning out thousands of pages of crusading sermons, fulminating pamphlets— even many hymns— during his 62 years. He wrote so much he is credited with helping shape the modern German language. Some of these writings were the doubtful, occasionally anti-Semitic musings of a depressed ex-monk. ("However irreproachably I lived as a monk, I felt myself in the presence of God to be a sinner with a most unquiet conscience," he recalled late in life.) But his doubts led him to question much established wisdom. His 95 Theses were a powerful criticism of papal excess. They not only set off scores of religious movements known collectively as Protestantism but eventually led to a reformed Roman Catholic Church. In embracing a view that "faith alone"—not works and certainly not papal indulgences—could bring salvation, he propelled the ordinary individual to the heart of religion, urging each soul to think about its own status before God.

Copernicus (1473-1543)
Astronomer of the Century

Fame would provide Niclas Kopernik's name with the weight of Latin, as if the sonorous tenor of antique sages were needed to embellish the genius of a boy born in Torun, Poland. Orphaned at 10, he was raised by his uncle, the Prince-Bishop of Ermland, and pointed toward service in the Catholic Church. But the bishop also sent his gifted nephew to his old school in Italy in 1497. And it was in Bologna that a mathematics professor inspired Niclas to question medieval astronomical dogma. It held that the universe was geocentric, with a stationary, motionless Earth placed at the center of several concentric, rotating spheres, each of which bore either a single planet, the sun, or all the stars. Returning to Poland, Kopernik pondered the strange motions of Mars, Jupiter and Saturn,

which sometimes appear to halt and reverse their travels through the sky. His startling conclusion: the so-called retrograde motion could be best explained by a heliocentric universe. In this revision of the cosmos, the stars and planets, including Earth, revolved around the sun. And our planet rotated daily on its axis. Thus a man moved the world—with numbers.

SCARY PRINCE
The romance of Don Carlos has become opera and drama: the idealistic heir to Spain is betrothed to a French princess until his grim father, the King, decides to wed her himself. Reality was uglier: the prince was mad and homicidal. Philip II had him locked up in a tower where Carlos slept naked on blocks of ice and eventually died of neglect—or suicide.

SCARIER PRINCE
For the good of the country, a ruler, wrote Niccolò Machiavelli, left, in *The Prince*, should "know how to enter evil," his success depending on "cruelties badly used or well used." *The Prince* was dedicated to the Medici duke Lorenzo II, but its ruthless tenets were practiced best (or worst) by a Medici princess: Lorenzo's daughter Catherine, Queen Mother of France.

Isaac Newton
(1642-1727)

His scientific search for a grand design in the universe overturned long-held assumptions

By LANCE MORROW

Standing in an unstable universe where distances contract and clocks slow down, and time and space are plastic, Albert Einstein cast a wistful backward glance at Isaac Newton. "Fortunate Newton, happy childhood of science!" the physicist wrote. "Nature to him was an open book, whose letters he could read without effort."

A child's first tasks are to walk and talk and understand his little universe. Newton, the 17th century's formidable prodigy, simply enlarged the project. The first of his family of Lincolnshire yeomen to be able to write his name, Newton grew into a touchy, passionately focused introvert who could go without sleep for days and live on bread and wine, and, at an astonishingly precocious age, absorbed everything important that was known to science up to that time (the works of Aristotle and, after that, the new men who superseded him: Copernicus, Kepler, Descartes and Galileo, who died in 1642, the year Newton was born). Riding on the shoulders of giants—and correcting them where they went wrong—Newton began assembling and perfecting the Newtonian universe, a miraculously predictable and rational clockwork creation held together by his universal gravitation and regulated by his elegant laws of motion.

Amazingly, the bulk of Newton's formative thought was accomplished at 23 and 24, while he was rusticated to Lin-

REMAINS OF THE DAY

MOST INFLUENTIAL ESSAYIST
John Locke's writings, including *An Essay Concerning Human Understanding*, expounded on the rights to revolution, liberty and the pursuit of happiness.

MOST PITHY PHILOSOPHY
René Descartes' eureka was *cogito, ergo sum*—"I think, therefore I am." It is the key link in his philosophy of deductive reasoning, mind/body dualism, the proof of God and the dream of medicine leading to physical immortality.

have seen *further,* it is by standing upon the shoulders of *Giants.*"

(1743-1826)

Thomas Jefferson

A political visionary's "expression of the American mind" still inspires rebels with a cause

By LANCE MORROW

Of America's Founding Fathers, Thomas Jefferson has fared the worst at the hands of revisionists. If he has managed to keep his place on Mount Rushmore, he has been vilified almost everywhere else in recent years as a slave-owning hypocrite and racist; a political extremist; an apologist for the vicious, botched French Revolution; and in general, somewhat less the genius remembered in our folklore than a provincial intellectual and tinkerer.

The onslaught is unfair. But even ardent Jeffersonians admit that the man was an insoluble puzzle. The contradictions in his character and his ideas could be breathtaking. That the author of the Declaration of Independence ("All men are created equal") not only owned and worked slaves at Monticello but also may have kept one of them, Sally Hemings, as a mistress—allegedly fathering children with her but never freeing her or them—was merely the most dramatic of his inconsistencies.

The brilliant American icon gets overtaken from time to time by his own apparent incoherence, his strangeness. He kept minutely detailed account books, for example—he was an obsessive record keeper who made daily notes on everything from barometric readings to the progress of 29 varieties of vegetables at Monticello—yet he somehow lost track of his debts and died bankrupt. The historian

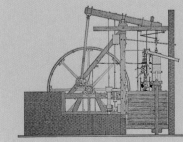

REMAINS OF THE DAY

BEST REVOLUTIONARY MACHINE
James Watt's single action steam engine, patented in 1769, revolutionized industry and spawned even more machinery to spur productivity.

WORST REVOLUTIONARY MACHINE
The guillotine, named for Joseph-Ignace Guillotin, a proponent of humane execution, was built by piano maker Tobias Schmidt. By the Reign of Terror's end, it had claimed 2,585 victims, including King Louis XVI and his queen, Marie Antoinette.

Paul Johnson has catalogued his inconsistencies: Jefferson was an élitist who disliked élites; a humorless man whose favorite books were *Don Quixote* and *Tristram Shandy;* a soft-spoken intellectual given to violent, inflammatory language ("The tree of liberty must be refreshed from time to time with the blood of patriots and tyrants") that in our day gets quoted by paranoiacs holed up in the Idaho mountains. Both liberals and conservatives claim him as their own.

WHAT DOES IT MEAN TO BE A JEFFERSONIAN? You must pick your Jefferson. Every other U.S. statesman, Henry Adams wrote, could be portrayed "with a few broad strokes of the brush," but Jefferson "only touch by touch with a fine pencil, and the perfection of the likeness depended upon the shifting and uncertain flicker of semitransparent shadows." Alas, indignant—or prurient—revisionism does not work with a fine pencil. Thomas Jefferson amounted to something infinitely more important—and more interesting—than one would know from the noise and scandal obscuring his achievement now.

He was arguably the most accomplished man (and in some ways the most fascinating one) who ever occupied the White House—naturalist, lawyer, educator, musician, architect, geographer, inventor, scientist, agriculturalist, philologist and more. His only presidential rival in versatility of intellect was Theodore Roosevelt. A magnificent writer and tireless correspondent, he left behind an astonishing 18,000 letters, including his memorable correspondence with John Adams. (The two men died on the same day, July 4, 1826, the 50th anniversary of the Declaration of Independence.)

Jefferson was a creature of the 18th century; he was *the* man of the 18th century. A dozen powerful strands of the Enlightenment converged in him: a certain sky-blue clarity, an aggressive awareness of the world, a fascination with science, a mechanical vision of the universe (much thanks to Isaac Newton) and an obsession with mathematical precision. The writer Garry Wills has suggested that Jefferson believed human life could be geared to the precision and simplicity of heaven's machinery. Many of the contradictions in his character arose from the discrepancies between such intellectual machinery and the passionate, organic disorders of life.

Jefferson's finest hour came when he was young, only 33. The Continental Congress, meeting in Philadelphia in June 1776, chose a committee of five, including Benjamin Franklin, Adams and Jefferson, to draft a Declaration of Independence. Jefferson nominated Adams to compose the draft. Adams demurred, "I am obnoxious, suspected and unpopular. You are very much otherwise." Besides, "you can write 10 times better than I." The committee agreed.

The truths that Jefferson famously declared to be "self-evident" were not new. He drew his ideas from an extraordinarily wide range of reading, especially from the works of Francis Bacon, Newton and John Locke, and from the Scottish moral philosophers—David Hume, Adam Smith. Some have dismissed the Declaration as merely eloquent propaganda—a sort of fancy mission statement for an insurrection. The only response is to observe the power of language to alter history. Jefferson explained, "I did not consider it as any part of my charge to invent new ideas altogether ... It was intended to be an expression of the American mind."

The work of a life may transcend the biography; a civilized person, the slave-owning hypocrite—or whatever he may have been beneath the impenetrable enamels of his character—formulated, in the Declaration of Independence, the founding aspiration of America and what is still its best self, an ideal that retains its motive force precisely because it is unfulfilled and maybe unfulfillable.

In later years, he learned that democracy could be distorted from Republican France and Napoleon (a "wretch," Jefferson charged, of "maniac ambition"). Jefferson stitched together popular sovereignty and liberty, all under divine sponsorship and legitimized by ancient precedent and English tradition. Writes historian Merrill Peterson: "For the first time in history, 'the rights of man,' not of rulers, were laid at the foundation of a nation. The first great Colonial revolt perforce became the first great democratic revolution as well." With the Declaration, Jefferson gave the Enlightenment its most eloquent and succinct political expression. He lifted the human race into a higher orbit. ∎

BEST PROPHET
Capitalist guru Adam Smith, left, author of *The Wealth of Nations,* predicted that America, then in rebellion against Britain, and other "empty continents" would be the brave new models of a mercantilist world.

BEST VILLAGE PHILOSOPHER
He claimed a grandparent from faraway Scotland, but Immanuel Kant, left, was a stay-at-home who spent almost all his life in Königsberg, east Prussia (now Kaliningrad, Russia). His reputation for sagacity exerted such pull that pilgrims of philosophy flocked to Königsberg to hear him speak.

An Age of Revolutionaries

The forces unleashed by the Enlightenment inspired a generation of rebels to reshape the world they inherited

Benjamin Franklin (1706-1790)
Savant of the Century

In order to understand Benjamin Franklin's historic significance, we must first rescue him from the schoolbook stereotype: a sage geezer flying kites in the rain and lecturing us about a penny saved being a

penny earned. His experiments with electricity led him to invent the lightning rod, devise the theory of positive and nega- tive charges, name the battery and become one of his century's foremost scientists. As for his *Poor Richard's Almanac* adages, they made him not only a best-selling author but also the first Ameri- can media mogul: printer, editor, publisher, newspaper franchiser and consolidator and controller of the first great distribu- tion network—the postal service. His inventions included the Franklin stove and the bifocal lens. As a statesman, he played a key role in America's four founding documents and was the only person to sign them all: the Declaration of Independence (he edited Jefferson's draft), the treaty of alliance with France (which he negotiated), the peace treaty ending the Revolution (which he negotiated) and the Constitution (he came up with the idea of a House representing the people and a Senate representing the states).

Ludwig van Beethoven (1770-1827)
Composer of the Century

His art soared with drama and pathos; his life met with debilitation and despair. Ludwig van Beethoven was born in Bonn, the son of a tempestuous father who raised his talented son to succeed Mozart and then drank himself to death. Beethoven's early compo- sitions were for piano; his performances throughout Europe earned him acclaim as an improviser. But he was plagued with hearing problems, and after suffering a prolonged bout of depression, he relocated to a rural village outside Vienna and sought relief in composing. He found the solace he wanted and produced, over the next decade, a wealth of glorious, enduring symphonic works. The music, bridging the catastrophic finale of the old century of his birth and the febrile promise of a new era, had the whiff of

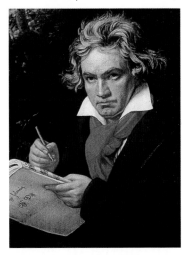

revolution: it destroyed the classical symphonic molds and established a new era of Romanticism. Even as his hearing worsened, sending him alternately into fits of despair and manic frenzy, Beethoven continued to create art of astonishing uplift.

BEST MUSICAL PRODIGY
Johann Chrysostom Wolfgang Amadeus Mozart, right, to give him his full name, began composing music before he could write notes (his father Leopold transcribed them). By age 6, he was touring with his father and older sister Maria Anna; he was the musical wonder of the world by 10. In his short life he composed some of the most lyrical music ever written. But when he died in 1791, at 35, he was in great debt and was buried in a common grave.

LEAST APPRECIATED GENIUS
The music of Johann Sebastian Bach got little respect in his lifetime. Critics called it "turgid and confused," excessively artful and not at all comparable to Handel's. After his death in 1750, some 100 of his sacred cantatas were lost. A cult of devotees kept his memory alive until Bach was "discovered" in the early 1800s.

His inventions helped reshape modernity— and promised a future bounded only by creativity

By PAUL GRAY

(1847-1931)

Thomas Edison

In 1926 the philosopher Alfred North White-head wrote, "The greatest invention of the 19th century was the invention of the method of invention." That method, White-head added, "has broken up the foundations of the old civilization." Yet Thomas Alva Edison never thought of himself as a revolutionary; he was a hardworking, thoroughly practical man, a

REMAINS OF THE DAY

ART FOR WHAT'S SAKE?
"Journalism is unreadable and literature is not read," Oscar Wilde, left, lamented. The literary center was held by Charles Dickens, right, and his reportorial novels, while Wilde led the aesthetes. Like Tom Wolfe vs. John Updike today— (with Wolfe in Wilde's clothing).

1000 MILE
ENDURANCE RUN
BAILEY ELECTRIC
NEW EDISON
STORAGE BATTERY

Electric Touch-Control
FOR THE DICTATOR

Edison's Latest Invention
THE ELECTRIP EDIPHON

Phonograph

EDISON'S
ELECTRIC PEN and PRESS
5000
COPIES FROM A SINGLE WRITING.

Experiment No. 1.   Feby 13 1880

Small horseshoe

problem solver who cared little about ideas for their own sake. But he was also the most prodigious inventor of his era, indeed of all time, and he was recognized as the spirit of a new age by his contemporaries. They observed the amazing new products streaming out of his New Jersey laboratory and, sensing magic, named Edison the Wizard of Menlo Park.

The inventor's magic had nothing to do with illusions: it was driven by exhaustive research and a tenacious unwillingness to quit tinkering until a technical challenge had been met. "Genius," he famously remarked, "is about 2% inspiration and 98% perspiration."

EDISON'S TIRELESS WORK HABITS WERE SHAPED BY his childhood in Michigan. His formal education lasted some three months; he quit school after a teacher called him "addled." His mother, herself a former teacher, educated him for a while at home, but the boy's growing fascination with chemistry led him into a rigorous course of independent study. To pay for research materials, Edison at age 12 got a job as a candy and newspaper vendor on a railroad. By the time he was 16, he had learned telegraphy and began working as an operator at various points in the Middle West; in 1868 he joined the Boston office of Western Union. Here he read Michael Faraday's Experimental Researches in Electricity and decided to become an inventor.

His first patent, for an electric vote recorder, taught him a lesson that would guide his career. There was no demand, at the time, for electric vote recorders, and his device earned him nothing. Edison vowed never again to invent something unless he could be sure it was marketable.

Fortunately for him, America during the post–Civil War boom of the 1870s was famished for faster and more reliable ways of doing business. An improvement Edison made in the stock ticker eventually earned him $40,000, a large sum at the time. With this windfall he set up and staffed a shop in Newark, N.J., to manufacture these tickers. But other companies began besieging Edison for technical advice, and in 1876 he relocated to Menlo Park, where he created the world's first industrial-research facility, a humming workplace dedicated to improving or creating new products for pay. Menlo Park itself, which showed the world a new method of making progress, was one of Edison's most influential inventions.

Other candidates for this honor soon abounded. Edison was working on a problem in telegraphy in 1877 when he noticed that a stylus drawn rapidly across the embossed symbols of the Morse code emitted "a light, musical, rhythmical sound, resembling human talk heard indistinctly." If it was possible, he reasoned, to "hear" dots and dashes, might not the human voice be reproduced in a similar manner? After much trial and error, Edison gathered a small group of witnesses and recited "Mary Had a Little Lamb" into a strange-looking device. The spectators were amazed to hear the machine play back Edison's high-pitched voice. The phonograph was born.

Edison is commonly called the inventor of the light bulb. In truth, he and his co-workers accomplished far more than that. In 1879 they created an incandescent lamp with a carbonized filament that would burn for 40 hours, but a working laboratory model was only the first step. How could they make this device illuminate the world? For this they would need a host of devices, including generators, motors, junction boxes, safety fuses and underground conductors, many of which did not exist. Amazingly, only three years later Edison opened the first commercial electric station on Pearl Street in lower Manhattan; it served roughly 85 customers with 400 lamps and pioneered the inexorable process of turning night into day.

Either alone or as the supervisor of his research teams, Edison amassed more than 1,000 patents, including one for the movie camera. That invention alone would have ensured his lasting renown, but it was only one of the many contributions he made to the now ubiquitous technological environment. He created the look and sound of contemporary life. Once, he was signing a guest book and came to the Interested In column. Edison wrote, "Everything." ∎

MOST INFECTIOUS TYRANT
Napoleonic egomania would inspire dictators well into the 20th century. Bonaparte gilded his legend with portraits, enigmatic anecdotes and iconic acts, like pushing aside the Pope to crown himself Emperor.

WOMEN IN AND OUT OF POWER
Britain's Queen Victoria, center, epitomized an age of plenty but assumed the throne in 1837 only because her uncle William IV died childless. China's Empress Dowager Cixi, right, was a mere concubine but acquired clout by bearing the Emperor his only son. Queen Liliuokalani of Hawaii, left, lost her kingdom to white sugar planters, who got the U.S. to annex it in 1898.

When Houses Were Divided

As Americans battled over the burdens of slavery, the theories of an English scientist rocked the Victorian world

Abraham Lincoln (1809-1865)
Conscience of the Century

By conventional standards, no American President was more ill prepared for the job. Raised poor in Kentucky and Indiana, Lincoln finished barely a year

of formal schooling. But his ambition, pragmatism and generosity of spirit catapulted him into politics at a time when the nation was riven by slavery and looming secession. He opposed the spread of slavery to the Western states; in 1860, pledging to save the Union, he was elected President. During the Civil War he showed himself to be a shrewd military tactician and a leader of surpassing moral courage. With the signing of the Emancipation Proclamation in 1863, he expanded the war's purpose, making it nothing less than a fight for freedom and the survival of democracy. He became convinced that slavery was a sin shared by North and South that had to be cleansed on the battlefield. "If God wills that it continue ... until every drop of blood drawn with the lash shall be paid by another drawn with the sword," he said, "so it still must be said, 'the judgments of the Lord are true and righteous altogether.'" America's greatest President paid for that faith with his own life.

Charles Darwin (1809-1882)
Iconoclast of the Century

Charles Darwin didn't want to murder God, as he once put it. But he did. He didn't want to defy his fellow Cantabrigians, his gentlemanly Victorian society, his devout wife. But he did. He waited 20 years to publish his theory of natural selection, but—fittingly, after another scientist threatened to be first—he did. Before Darwin, most people accepted some version of biblical creation. Humans were seen as the apotheosis of godly architecture. But on his voyage on H.M.S. *Beagle,* Darwin saw that species on different islands had developed differently. Humans could thus be an accident of natural selection, not a direct product of God. "The subject haunted me," he later wrote. (In fact, worries about how much his theory would shake society exacerbated the strange illnesses he suffered.) Darwin's theories still provoke opposition. One hundred and forty years after *The Origin of Species,* backers of creationism still fight to keep evolution out of schools. Yet Darwinism remains one of the most successful scientific theories ever promulgated. Hardly an element of humanity—not capitalism, not gender relations, certainly not biology—can be fully understood without its help.

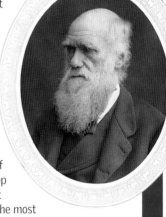

MOST SHAPELY PAINTER
Impressionism begat Cubism as Paul Cézanne rendered the world "in terms of the cylinder, the sphere, the cone."

BEST DOCTOR
Louis Pasteur's medical breakthroughs saved countless lives—and helped dairy farmers and brewers ensure the safety of their products.

POOR PROPHET
Karl Marx: "Capitalist production begets, with the inexorability of a law of nature, its own negation." But he didn't say when.

Index

Index

Photo Credits

Photo credits read left to right and from top to bottom of page, except as noted.

Cover

Photo-illustration by Sanjay Kothari, Churchill by Yousuf Karsh—Woodfin Camp, Map by The Stock Market, Atom by Gilbert—Photo Researchers, Diana by John Stilwell—PA, Armstrong by Eliot Elisofon—LIFE©Time Inc., Model T by Ford Motor Company, Picasso by Edward Quinn—Camera Press/Retna, Vietnam by Eddie Adams—AP—Wide World Photos, F.D.R. by George Skadding—LIFE, Fiber Optics by Hamblin—Gamma Liaison, Dolly by Chris Buck—Corbis Outline, Hitler by Archive Photos, 3-D Theater by J.R. Eyerman—LIFE©Time Inc.

Contents

iv Mansell Collection—Time Inc., Reuters—Corbis Bettmann, Bob Gomel—LIFE, AFF—AFS **v** Tim O'Brien (3), C.F. Payne

Heroes & Icons

1 no credit, J.P. Laffont—Corbis Sygma, AP—Wide World Photos **2-3** Illustrations by Luba Lukova **4** W. Eugene Smith—LIFE **5** U.S. Army Signal Corps, Robert Capa—Magnum Photos **6** Larry Burrows—LIFE **7** David Douglas Duncan—Harry Ransom Humanities Research Center, U. of Texas at Austin, David Turnley—Corbis **8** Corbis Bettmann, Lindberg Picture Collection—Yale University Library **9** Culver Pictures **10** Culver Pictures **11** Corbis Hulton Deutsch Collection, AP—Wide World Photos, U.S. Air Force, Corbis Bettmann **12** ©Royal Geographic Society **13** Topham Picturepoint—The Imageworks **14** The New Studio—Katmandu, ©Royal Geographic Society **15** Hulton Getty—Liaison, Lomen Family Collection—University of Alaska, Wide World Photos, National Archives **16** Archives Tallandier—Sipa, AFF—AFS—Archive **17** Illustration by Lauren Uram **18** AFF—AFS—Archive **19** Pix Inc.—Time Inc. **20** Culver Pictures, Corbis Bettmann **21** Culver Pictures, Nina Leen—LIFE **22** J.P. Laffont—Corbis Sygma **23** Raghu Rai—Magnum Photos, Atlan—Corbis Sygma **24** Raghu Rai—Magnum Photos **25** no credit, D. Farber—Corbis Sygma, C. Bachelier—Corbis Sygma, David Gahr **26** Hoepker—Magnum Photos **27** Howard Bingham, AP—Wide World Photos **28** Howard Bingham (2) **29** Neil Leifer **30** Nikolas Muray Photo Archive—Nikolas Muray, Brett Wills—Courtesy Hockey Hall of Fame, Hulton Getty—Liaison, no credit, George Silk—LIFE **31** Corbis Bettmann, Neil Leifer, Yale Joel—LIFE, Walter Iooss Jr.—Griededieck—SPORTS ILLUSTRATED **32** Corbis Bettmann **33** Bob Wheeler—LIFE **34** AP—Wide World Photos, Courtesy of Rachel Robinson **35** Art Seitz—Liaison, New York *Daily News*, Corbis Bettmann, Tom Hauck—Allsport **36** AP—Wide World Photos **37** Peter Robinson—Empics Ltd. **38** Popperfoto **39** Illustration by Charles Burns **40** Globe Photos, Lou Valentino Collection **41** no credit, Doris Nieh—Globe Photos **42** ©1999 Archives of Milton H. Greene, LLC. All Rights Reserved www.archivesmhg.com **44** George Zeno Collection, Richard C. Miller—MPTV **45** George Zeno Collection, Eve Arnold—Magnum Photos **46** Patrick Lichfield—Camera Press—Retna, Camera Press—Retna **47** Snowdon—Camera Press—Retna **48** Patrick Demarchelier—Camera Press—Retna **49** De Keerle—Gamma Liaison, Courtesy The Ronald Reagan Library, Tim Graham—Sygma **50** MPTV (2) **51** Dana Fineman—Corbis Sygma, Keystone, MPTV, Kobal Collection **52** Michael O'Neill—Corbis Outline, Kobal Collection **53** MPTV (2), Lance Staedler—Corbis Outline, Kobal Collection **54** John F. Kennedy Library **56** Toni Frissel—John F. Kennedy Library, Stanley Tretick—Corbis Sygma **57** Ed Clark—LIFE, John F. Kennedy Library, Arnaldo Magnani—Gamma Liaison **58** Hulton Getty—Liaison **59** Press Association, Corbis Bettmann **60** Hulton Getty—Liaison **61** Brian Lanker **62** Corbis Bettmann, AP—Wide World Photos **63** Don Cravens—LIFE **64** Thomas McAvoy—LIFE, Stuart Franklin—Corbis Sygma, John Launois—Black Star, Corbis **65** Paul Fusco—Magnum Photos **66** Susan Ehmer—San Francisco *Chronicle*, AP—Wide World Photos **67** Terry Schmidt—San Francisco *Chronicle* **68** Andres Chiong, Bolivia Embassy—AP—Wide World Photos **69** Illustration by Edel Rodriguez **70** AP—Wide World Photos

71 Susan Meiselas—Magnum Photos, Yankelevich—Sipa Press **72** Yousuf Karsh—Woodfin Camp **73** Itar—TASS—Sovfoto **75** Leviton-Atlanta, AP—Wide World Photos **76** Bernard Gotfryd—Woodfin Camp **77** Gregory Heisler for TIME **78** Courtesy The Wilson House **79** A.A. World Services Inc. **80** Courtesy The Wilson House

Person of the Century

81 Lotte Jacobi Archive—University of New Hampshire, Kamu Gandhi, Corbis Bettmann **82-89** Illustrations by Luba Lukova **82** Eastfoto—Sovfoto **83** Corbis Bettmann, Edward Quinn—Camera Press—Retna, Paul Conklin—Pix Inc.—Time Inc. **84** Kamu Gandhi **87** George Skadding—LIFE **89** Corbis Bettmann **91** Painting for TIME by Tim O'Brien **92** Lotte Jacobi Archive—University of New Hampshire, California Institute of Technology—Einstein Archives, Hulton Deutsch Collection—Corbis **93** Yousuf Karsh—Woodfin Camp **95** Albert Einstein Archives—Hebrew University Jerusalem **96-97** Lotte Jacobi Archive—University of New Hampshire **98** Acme—Corbis Bettmann **99** Mansell Collection—Time Inc. **100** Eric Schaal—Time-Life Syndication **102** Hansel Meith—LIFE **104** Eliot Elisofon—LIFE **105** UPI—Corbis Bettmann **107** Painting for TIME by Tim O'Brien **108** Franklin D. Roosevelt Library **109** Harris & Ewing Photos **110** Franklin D. Roosevelt Library **111** Peter Stackpole—LIFE **112** Corbis Bettmann **113** Margaret Suckley **114** Wide World Photos **115** Ed Clark **117** Painting for TIME by Tim O'Brien **118** Camera Press—Pix Inc. **119** D.R.D. Wadia **120** Margaret Bourke-White—LIFE **121** AP—Wide World Photos, Margaret Bourke-White—LIFE **122** AP—Wide World Photos **123** Louise Gubb—The Image Works **124** Len Lahman—Los Angeles *Times*, Dennis Brack—Black Star, David Turnley—Corbis **125** Don Farber—Corbis Sygma, Robin Moyer, Charles Moore—Black Star **127** Heinrich Hoffmann—TIME Syndication **128** Sam Gilbert—U.S. Army—National Archives

People of the Millennium

130 P. Anderson—The Anawakali Museum, The Tokubawa Art Museum **131** Painting for TIME by Jack Unruh **132** Granger Collection, Dmitri Kessel—LIFE **133** Angelo Hornak—Corbis, ©Archivo Iconografico, S.A.—Corbis, Erich Lessing—AKG Photo (2) **134** The Mansell Collection—Time Inc. **135** Painting for TIME by Kinuko Craft **136** Werner Forman—Corbis, Mark Tuschman **137** The Bridgeman Art Gallery, National Gallery of Art, Washington, D.C., The Mansell Collection—Time Inc. (2) **138** Granger Collection, The Goldsmith's Company **139** Painting for TIME by Chang Park **140** Corbis Bettmann, Marc Garanger—Corbis **141** Margaritone D'Arezzo—The Vatican Art Collection, Granger Collection, no credit, Culver Pictures **142** The Bridgeman Art Library **143** Painting for TIME by Mario Donizetti **144** no credit, The Mansell Collection—Time Inc. **145** AFP, Granger Collection, The Metropolitan Museum of Art **146** Granger Collection **147** Artwork for TIME by Lauren Uram **148** Granger Collection (2) **149** Granger Collection, Snark—Art Resource, The Bridgeman Art Gallery **150** The Mansell Collection—Time Inc., ©Gianni Dagliort—Corbis **151** Painting for TIME by David Bowers **152** no credit, Rafael/Uffizi—Alinari/Art Resource, Scala—Art Resource **153** Lucas Cranach The Elder/Museo Poldi Pezzoli—Scala, Corbis Bettmann, Palazzo Vecchio/Scala—Art Resource **154** National Portrait Gallery-London, The Mansell Collection—Time Inc. **155** Artwork for TIME by Mark Summers **156** Granger Collection, The New York Public Library **157** Uffizi—Scala, Royal Shakespeare Company, Granger Collection **158** Granger Collection, Leonard de Selva—Corbis **159** Painting for TIME by C.F. Payne **160** The Bridgeman Art Gallery, AKG Berlin **161** National Portrait Gallery/Smithsonian Institution/Art Resource NY, Granger Collection (2) **162** N. Sarnoy—Library of Congress, Corbis Bettmann **163** Artwork for TIME by Amy Guip **164** ©Archivo Iconografico S.A.—Corbis, Corbis-Bettmann, Granger Collection, Courtesy of Ernst Von Harringa **165** no credit, The Mansell Collection—Time Inc., Courtesy Kunstmuseum-Bern, Granger Collection, Corbis Bettmann